WE HAD INK IN OUR BLOOD

© 2020 edited by Terry Nau and R. Thomas Berner
Printed in the United States of America

All rights reserved. This publication is protected by Copyright, and permission should be obtained from the publisher prior to any prohibited reproduction, storage in a retrieval system, or transmission in any form or by any means, electronic, mechanical, photocopying, recording, or likewise.

Published by Mt. Nittany Press, an imprint of Eifrig Publishing,
PO Box 66, Lemont, PA 16851.

For information regarding permission, write to:

Rights and Permissions Department,
Eifrig Publishing,
PO Box 66, Lemont, PA 16851, USA.
permissions@eifrigpublishing.com, 888-340-6543.

Library of Congress Cataloging-in-Publication Data

We Had Ink in our Blood: Newspaper Memories from Former CDT, Pa. Mirror Staffers

by Terry Nau and R. Thomas Berner
p. cm.
Paperback: ISBN 978-1-63233-261-5
Hardcover: ISBN 978-1-63233-262-2
Ebook: ISBN 978-1-63233-263-9

1. Media--Newspaper 2. Centre County (Pa.)--History]
I. Nau, Terry and R. Thomas Berner. II. Title

24 23 22 21 20
5 4 3 2 1
Printed in the USA on recycled paper.

WE HAD INK IN OUR BLOOD

Newspaper Memories from Former CDT, Pa. Mirror Staffers

Co-edited by Terry Nau and
R. Thomas Berner

LEMONT

Acknowledgments

This book is dedicated to former Pennsylvania Mirror and Centre Daily Times sportswriter Dennis Gildea, who died on May 3, 2020, after a hard fight with brain cancer. Our thanks to his wife, Constance Wicklund Gildea, for allowing us to use personal photos of Dennis in the book.

In addition, we would like to thank CDT Publisher Janet Santostefano, Executive Editor Jessica McAllister and Managing Editor Lauren Muthler for granting us permission to use an archived news story by Bill Welch.

We also want to acknowledge a few key figures from both newspapers who have died over the years, including J. E. Holtzinger, Paul Houck, Jerry Weinstein, Bill Welch, Sheila Irvine, Bob Trump, Chance Conner and John Andrews, the unofficial sports editor of the Mirror. Sadly, the list is longer than that but these are among the folks mentioned in the book. We can also recall the loss of Gene Reilly, John Brutzman, Joan Kurilla, Kathleen Ewing, Paul Poorman, Terry Dalton, Paul Dubbs, Jack Yeager, Elliot Potter, James Snyder, and Molly (nee Yeager) Blakeslee.

Co-editors Terry Nau and R. Thomas Berner would like to thank all of our former colleagues who have contributed chapters to this book. They include Ron Bracken, Gary Tuma, Glenn Sheeley, Don Black, Greg Guise, Bob Emmers, Denise Bowman-Scott, Perri Foster-Pegg Capell, Bill Horlacher, Chris Koll, Sara Pitzer, Dave Baker, Dave Cuzzolina and Dave Bloss. Not to mention Thomazine Weinstein Shanahan and Jim Houck, who wrote beautiful chapters about their fathers.

Special thanks from Terry Nau to Tom Berner for his historical perspective and editing skills. Tom worked for both newspapers and then went on to a long career teaching journalism at Penn State. If you see any typos, they're my fault!

~ Terry Nau

Table of Contents

Prologue   7
Turning a Movie into a Book

Chapter 1   11
A Two-Newspaper Town

Chapter 2   23
Paul Houck Aimed for the Moon

Chapter 3   38
Jerry Weinstein: The Man Who Was the CDT

Chapter 4   46
Ron Bracken: "Who Are Those guys?"

Chapter 5   54
Terry Nau: Work Hard, Play Hard

Chapter 6   69
Don Black: Photojournalist to Publisher

Chapter 7   78
Greg Guise: From Bedford to Berlin

Chapter 8   85
Robert Emmers: Hooked by a Byline

Chapter 9 103
Bill Welch: Lights Out at Hoy Brothers

Chapter 10 108
Gary Tuma: So This is Journalism?

Chapter 11 125
Glenn Sheeley: My Favorite Year

Chapter 12 135
Denise Bowman-Scott: Don't Get Married and Leave!

Chapter 13 143
Perri Foster-Pegg: How the Mirror Saved My Life

Chapter 14 154
Bill Horlacher: Gone But Not Forgotten

Chapter 15 159
Chris Koll: The Wrestling Sportswriter

Chapter 16 164
Sara Pitzer: Feature Writer and Farmer

Chapter 17 172
Dave Baker: The Stat Man Cometh

Chapter 18 180
Dave Cuzzolina: The Mirror Shatters

Chapter 19 191
Dave Bloss: These Were Good People

Epilogue: 201
R. Thomas Berner: The Eulogy

PROLOGUE: TURNING A MOVIE INTO A BOOK

Why would a bunch of retired newspaper people want to team up to write a book about the first full-time job most of them ever had? Hopefully, the answer lies in the chapters that follow this prologue. We all wrote our memories while sheltering in during the Great Pandemic of 2020. If ever there were a time to be reflective and look back on our youthful days, that spring was the moment.

My own desire to dig out these memories came from the sudden illness last summer of our friend and colleague, Dennis Gildea, to whom this book is dedicated. Whenever we had a few beers, Dennis would invariably mention that we should write a movie screenplay about the Pennsylvania Mirror's short life. He said it would begin with the sound of screeching tires as I crashed my new Camaro into a creek in Pine Grove Mills back in 1973.

"Just roll the opening credits right there," Dennis would say. "Rain coming down in buckets. And Nay-You (Dennis's way of butchering my last name) getting out of the car, standing on the roof, and telling the innocent bystanders, 'No applause, please.' And then we tell the story of the Pennsylvania Mirror, from start to finish, nine glorious years."

GOOD IDEA –
Dennis Gildea never took life too seriously. (Photo courtesy of Bill "Sneeks" Scutta)

Our conversation never went any further because life got in the way. Plus, who knew how to write a screenplay? Not us. Once I retired, though, I found out how easy it is to self-publish paperback books. I wrote five on the Vietnam War, mostly oral histories, using my newspaper skills to interview Vietnam veterans about that exciting time in their lives, when the adrenalin flowed every day. When we were 20 years old.

The Mirror came a few years later for me, when I was almost 25. I had already met Dennis through my work at the Daily Collegian. In the next five years, I would meet almost all of the folks who have contributed to this book, which evolved from a tale of the Pennsylvania Mirror to the story of its short-lived battle to survive against the Centre Daily Times, which scored a stunning knockout in the ninth year of the fight. (The CDT was winning easily on points when the Mirror threw in the towel.)

You look at the list of writers in this book and it is a testimony to the talent at both papers. The CDT's Ron Bracken was a rival and friend who won so many awards for his writing that he stopped counting. Gary Tuma also worked for the CDT. He shared a rental house with me for two years in the mid-1970s before we both got out of town. We were all interconnected somehow. Gary makes the point that the two rival sports departments got along well, even as we tried to outshine the other.

Tom Berner worked at both newspapers, the Mirror and the CDT, before going on to a long career at Penn State as a journalism professor. Dave Bloss, who writes the final chapter in this book, is an old friend who intuitively knows what I am thinking. Dave took on the job of saying goodbye to our friend Dennis over the past year, which was hard for him, and for Dennis's wife, Constance Wicklund Gildea, or "CW," as Dennis often called her.

We have chapters in this book written by the son and daughter of the two newsroom leaders, Paul Houck and Jerry Weinstein. I wanted those chapters up front because Paul and Jerry deserve to be there. Jim Houck and Timmy Weinstein Shanahan did their fathers proud.

Bob Emmers also worked at both papers and presents a compelling story of his experiences. Two Mirror photographers, Don Black and Greg Guise, went far in their careers, both in distance traveled and in experiences gained. Don had a photo nominated for the Pulitzer Prize and Greg covered the fall of the Berlin Wall, modestly observing that he was usually working in the CBS production truck, two blocks away.

Women journalists had to put up with a lot in the 1970s. Denise Bowman-Scott writes a straight-forward account of her early days in journalism. Perri Foster-Pegg Capell tells how a job at the Mirror saved her life. Sara Pitzer recalls a humorous tale of "women's page" adventures and her life as a farmer in Rebersburg.

Let's not forget Chris Koll, the wrestling sportswriter, and Dave Baker, who sent in Little League box scores to CDT sports editor Doug McDonald from Gill Field in State College. Dave went on to become a great "stat man" and is currently an assistant athletic director at Penn State.

Dave Cuzzolina, who had the thankless task of guiding the Mirror over its final 18 months, agreed to write a chapter for this book, and admitted that it was fun to recall the excitement of newspaper work, which he left a decade later. Dave never forgot the newsroom sound of bells ringing whenever a major story came across the AP wire machine. Three bells meant a solid story was moving across the wire. Four bells might require immediate attention. Five bells? Elvis Presley's death in August 1977 got five bells. Everyone present in the newsroom came running to the wire room to see what happened. We saw the news occur in real time. None of us ever got over the excitement that sometimes broke out in a newsroom. What other profession keeps you informed of world, national and community events while you are working?

My only regret is not having chapters from Dennis Gildea, Dave Fay and John Andrews, who have all died. We write about them in several chapters. They were the heart and soul of the Mirror in the 1970s. I could say the same for the late Bill Welch, who went from reporter to executive editor of the CDT, a wonderful writer whose story of the Hoy Brothers store closing in 1973 evokes a different time in the world that was State College in the 1950s and 1960s. The best part of this book is paying tribute to these old friends, and to our former bosses, Paul Houck and Jerry Weinstein.

But it all comes back to Dennis Gildea. He taught me to never take life too seriously. And I didn't, until we got older and realized that the best time in our newspaper lives may have occurred back in the 1970s in a college town sealed off from the rest of the world. We all went on to different challenges over the next 43 years, never really forgetting the place where we learned the business of reporting and editing.

So we settled for a book, Dennis. No movie credits rolling down the screen. Just words on a bunch of pages. Sit back, pour yourself a Utica Club, and enjoy the book.

~**Terry Nau**

CHAPTER 1
A TWO-NEWSPAPER TOWN

By R. Thomas Berner

(EDITOR'S NOTE: R. Thomas Berner worked on the original staff at the Pennsylvania Mirror before moving over to the Centre Daily Times in 1971. He left the newspaper business in 1975 to teach journalism at Penn State for 28 years.)

A Personal Prologue

I fell in love with newspapers when I was in senior high. Yes, I had looked at newspapers before that and had even been a paperboy (as they were called before the gender-neutral term "carrier" went into effect). But love came in my senior year when I realized that the only way I could get close to the girl I had a crush on was to join the staff of my high school newspaper.

She was the editor.

Alas, nothing came of the romance, but consider what it did for me. While still in high school, I became a stringer for my local newspaper in Tamaqua, the Evening Courier, and then, upon graduation, its only sportswriter. The publisher said he hired me partly on the strength of a recommendation from his next-door neighbor, who said I had a good work ethic.

The neighbor was, in one of those life coincidences, the editor of my high school newspaper. Although I never got to first base with the high school editor and haven't seen her since graduation

VERSATILE –
R. Thomas Berner worked at both the Pa. Mirror and the Centre Daily Times. (Photo courtesy of Paulette L. Berner)

day in 1961 (she became a missionary, and if you know me, you can see that would have never worked), I did end up with a great career because of the newspaper business.

A Two-Newspaper Town

On Dec. 11, 1968, State College, Pennsylvania, became one of the rarest post-1960 communities in the United States. It became a two-newspaper town. It was on that date that the Pennsylvania Mirror was born. The established newspaper was the Centre Daily Times, which had been born as a weekly in 1898 and had become a daily in 1934.

Newspaper history is filled with records of two and multiple newspaper towns. The bigger the metropolitan area, the more the newspapers, with New York City being the best example. In Pennsylvania many of the two-newspaper towns were merely morning and afternoon papers owned by the same family. Notable exceptions would be Philadelphia, Pittsburgh, Wilkes-Barre, Scranton and York. And then State College, which was the smallest municipality of any to have two newspapers.

The Mirror was born late in the early morning of Dec. 11, not because that was desired, but because the composing room could not paste up and deliver pages soon enough for the scheduled pressrun. Gerry Lynn Hamilton, then the city editor of the Daily Collegian, the student newspaper at Penn State, recalls having been given a tour of the new plant:

At the end of the tour, I expressed my appreciation. The Himes (Printing Company) gentleman asked if I had any newspaper experience. "Yes. A little," I answered. Then he asked if I would like a job. I was curious, and I asked when he wanted me to start. "Right now," was the answer.

I explained that I was a student on term break, but I could work for a week. We agreed. He took me back to the composing room and introduced me. Then I took off my jacket, loosened my tie, and started working. That was about 4 p.m.

I quickly discovered that the shop foreman and the assistant foreman had experience, but no other composing room employees did. I also discovered that the modern equipment was fussy and flaky. Sometime after midnight, someone came into the shop to have me fill out some paperwork and sign a time card. The details are fuzzy now, but I think I worked until about 5 a.m., when we finished the final page paste-ups. Shortly afterward — And well after deadline — the press run started. I got a copy hot off the press and went home.

I didn't get to grab a copy and go home. Instead, because I supposedly knew my way around the area, I was recruited to help a delivery truck driver get the bundles to the drop-off points. I rode shotgun with a map in hand. I think we dropped off the last bundle around 9 a.m. in Unionville. It was the first time I had ever been in Unionville.

But the names of towns in Centre County were not new to me. One of my pre-publication assignments was to type up the names of the towns from Centre County and the surrounding counties so the executive editor, Paul Houck (see Chapter 2), could create a front page that said (in multiple colors): Good Morning and listed the towns. I remember finding a town Houck, a Centre County native, didn't know about. I was delighted; so was he.

Even though I had just spent the summer between my freshman and sophomore year working at the Evening Courier in Tamaqua, the paper where I had gotten my start, I was not intending to work for another newspaper. I was at Penn State to go to law school (before Penn State even had a law school), but the G.I. Bill was not enough to support me and so I ended up at the Pennsylvania Mir-

PROUD MOMENT – *Mirror publisher Blair Bice, sports editor Dave Fay, executive editor Paul Houck and owner J.E. Holtzinger proudly display a Pennsylvania Newspaper Publisher Association award for best newspaper under 15,000 readers. (Pa. Mirror photo)*

ror. It wasn't long before I realized that I had ink in my veins and no interest in law school.[1]

The Mirror was different than the Courier. The printing technology, offset, allowed us to publish color photographs, and instead of setting type on bulky and slow-moving Linotype machines, our stories were keyboarded rapidly on tape and then run through a machine that produced the stories on glossy white paper that was run through a wax machine and then pasted onto the page. If you had no experience pasting up a page, it was a confusing process. Only after more experienced people were hired did we start to make deadline. In fact, the CDT that was published on our first day included an ad from the local typographers' union claiming that the CDT was the only paper put together by union

---

[1] Decades later I stumbled into a consulting gig as a journalism expert in defamation cases and after one case I was so glad I never went to law school.

printers. I don't think it mattered to CDT readers.

Houck designed a custom-made desk for reporters that ran almost the length of the newsroom and had positions for eight typewriters and phones. I don't ever remember eight reporters on the staff. We had a city editor and his assistant, a women's editor and her assistant, a business editor and one sports editor, all of whom had their own desks or offices. A plaque on display in the newsroom held a shovel with the words: THIS IS A SPADE; CALL IT THAT. Unlike the competition, we kowtowed to no one.

We felt that at the Centre Daily Penn State University was a sacred cow and the most sacred of cows was the football coach, Joe Paterno. The CDT used to run university news releases, which gave the impression that the CDT was covering campus events right and left. We used to put a tag on the releases identifying the university as the source so people knew where the news really came from.[2] I don't think it mattered to CDT readers.

How else did we try to distinguish ourselves from the gray CDT?

We were very aggressive — or tried to be — in our reporting. When West Beaver Avenue in State College was being rebuilt to bring it up to state standards for the implementation of the one-way traffic system, residents there complained that it was unsafe for their children to cross the street to go to school. We ran with that story day after day and the situation soon changed. Take that, CDT.

Shortly after the Mirror publication, a young woman named Judy Rife[3] joined the news staff and was assigned to cover Bellefonte. She was an excellent reporter. She had been covering a situation in which Bellefonte Borough was trying to purchase some property in the downtown. The owner wanted a lot of money, but the property wasn't worth it. Camera in hand, she trespassed on <u>the property</u> and produced a page of photographs accompanied

---

2 Fifty years later, given that a hollowed-out CDT staff produced so few local stories, I yearned for the old days.
3 She liked to point out that the New York Times wire service referred to the "penultimate graf" in a story. Not "penultimate paragraph," just "graf." "Only the Times would do something like that," she used to opine with a sigh.

15

by acid text noting that the buildings weren't worth much. They were vacant. You couldn't live in them. The owner threatened to sue but sold instead. A few years later when an extensive campaign was necessary to save a nearby mill the CDT's Terry Dalton did a great series that helped save the Gamble Mill. Dalton had replaced Bob Emmers (see Chapter 8), who had left for the Mirror.

In sports, thanks to the editor there, Dave Fay[4], we didn't write the usual morning stories in which the opening paragraph told you who won, who lost, when and the score. Fay insisted on feature leads to take away any chance of the CDT coming up with a more interesting story. Stories about games were not just dry recitations of who scored but became anecdotal and interesting. Fay once hired a PhD candidate and part-time bartender to take high school basketball box scores over the phone and reminded the fellow to get quotes from the coach. The first night on the job the fellow answered the phone from the coach this way: "Hi, coach, give me some quotes."[5] Fay was also talked Houck into subscribing to the AP's sportswire, which provided more extensive coverage and longer stories. Given all the space we had to fill, longer stories were needed. Unfortunately, we could not get the AP wirephoto service and relied on a package of photos delivered nightly to the bus station in State College. They were usually a day behind the news and so our local photographers were under a lot of pressure to provide lots of photographs. And we used them big.

Fay reminds me of one of my good headlines. He was covering Penn State in the Orange Bowl and had written a column about a closed practice for which his only source was a hot dog vendor outside the stadium. Of course, there was no vendor, but columnists have a lot of latitude. I headlined the column: Hot dog vendor peddles inside dope. The column won a prize and I frequently told Fay that it was the headline that did it. Without a good

---
4 Fay moved on and eventually landed at the Washington Times. He died in July 2007.
5 In the early 1970s after I had moved to the CDT, the Associated Press started sending optional feature leads on sports stories.

headline, I told Fay, the contest judge wouldn't have read it. Fay just rolled his eyes. I recall an even better headline three years later when I used a story on page one of the CDT that talked about a shortage of beef. That headline is my all-time favorite: Don't Beef: There Isn't Much.

Because we had so much space in the beginning, thanks to the paucity of advertisements, we gladly published public service ads for whatever charity sent them in. We needed them so badly we would paste one onto a page, photograph the page for the press and move the ad to another page.

We were always mindful that because of our advanced technology, we could print color easily and color photographs with a little more effort. The little more effort required that color photographs had to be processed in Altoona and someone in the newsroom had to be the courier.[6] The nameplate was blue and we used spot color as a backdrop for special stories.

Color photographs were another matter. For one, lighting was a problem. I remember photographer Les Shaw explaining that the lighting in Rec Hall was not friendly to color photography and the off-color results showed. Of course, you didn't need lights in Beaver Stadium because all games were played during the day, but even that changed over the years with televised night games.

The edict to think color did have some less than good results. One reporter talked the city editor into letting him do a story about the number of deer killed on Interstate 80 by trucks (usually) and cars. The story ran on page one with a color photograph of the reporter with a fresh deer carcass. The morning talk radio people had a field day with that one.

What really did not go well was the business model, at least as I understood it. Because our primary backers came from Altoona, we were not just a Centre County paper; we also circulated in Blair

---

[6] I volunteered several times just to get out of the office, but the downside was that you had to drive through Tyrone, which had an obnoxious smelling paper manufacturing plant that made one want to puke. I would gag from one end of town to the other.

County. That meant we had to have Blair County stories, which required us to replate the front page. That wasn't a problem. The problem was that we were not allowed to grow our circulation naturally toward Altoona, which was then a 45-mile trip on two-lane highways. We had to have a presence there almost immediately, and, I believe, it sapped our attention, our energy and our resources.

We did sell papers in Philipsburg in Centre County and even had a correspondent there who was ahead of her time. Among other things, she used a Polaroid camera to take a photo of the completion of Interstate 80. She drove it to our office, a trip of 30 miles on two-lane highway, and it was easy to make it bigger and use immediately. When I mentioned this later to the person in charge of the Associated Press in Pennsylvania, he said, in effect, that was the future, not the use of Polaroid cameras but a less cumbersome process getting photos delivered and published. Pre-computer, pre-attachment, pre-Photoshop.

Philipsburg presented another interesting situation. The publishers of the established newspapers had unwritten agreements not to encroach on each other's circulation area so the residents of Philipsburg never saw the CDT, but they were inundated with Pennsylvania Mirrors. One day a Philipsburg resident took an ad from the Mirror into a grocery chain in his town expecting to buy something at a special price and was surprised that the price in the Philipsburg store was higher than in the State College store where two or three chains competed along with several locally owned markets.

At the Mirror there was a lot of after-hours beer drinking. By my unprofessional analysis, the staff had three alcoholics. There were two affairs, one abortion, and one non-affair that a suspicious wife turned in to a beating of a young girl in the composing room. If the wife had only asked, she would have learned that the young girl had higher standards.

In the meantime, I was recruited by the CDT and started there in October 1971. Compared to the Mirror, the CDT was somnolent. The men wore coats and ties, went home to their wives after work and never caroused. They drank scotch, manhattans and martinis, and never more than one at night. The only affair I knew of led to marriage. And while the CDT did cover major municipal meetings, most of the township meetings came to us when a reporter called the recording secretary for information. We covered the faculty senate meetings at Penn State but I can assure you in hindsight as a future faculty senator, they were not as newsworthy as we made them out to be. Of course, both newspapers covered the antiwar demonstrations and the murder in the stacks of Pattee Library.

One of the great crusades taken on by our editor, Jerome Weinstein (see Chapter 3), was not just a successful push to get an open meetings law passed in Pennsylvania but to include the university's board of trustees in the law. As part of his overall crusade, he reprinted Florida's sunshine law. He urged readers to support the effort, making the valid point that open meetings were not for the benefit of the press alone but for anyone who wanted to attend.

The CDT had recruited me after two of its stars, Paul Dubbs and Jack Yeager, retired in the fall of 1971. Dubbs was the county editor, and Yeager, the associate editor and Weinstein's brother-in-law, covered Bellefonte and the courts. I became the city editor, although I think the original title was news editor. Bill Welch[7] moved up to managing editor; John Brutzman became the associate editor. Elliot Potter and Joan Kurilla also received titles but I doubt that anyone's paycheck changed.

While it was good for me professionally to move to the established daily, it was in one way a step back because the CDT was a letterpress newspaper just like the first one I had worked at in the early 60s. Producing it was time consuming. If you had overset stories, you heard about it, and if you didn't have enough type to

---

7 Welch died in September 2009. By then he had served as mayor of State College, a member of State College Borough Council , and editor of the American Philatelist, published by the American Philatelic Society

fill, you heard about it. It was a matter of efficiency and economics. You didn't want to waste anyone's time setting type that you might eventually have to throw away because the stories were out of date. Gauging the right amount was tricky.

It was a step back in time. At the Mirror, photographs were called art and the paper was assembled in the composing room, not the shop. The CDT was black and white, like that "old gray lady to the east" (as Welch dubbed it), the New York Times. Thanks to Weinstein, we had a better looking seven-column front page than the other Times, but inside we were the standard eight columns.

In my time (1971-75), I recall three above-average writers: Welch, Emmers and Dalton[8]. Weinstein used to complain that Welch was the best writer on the staff but he didn't write enough. Emmers produced at least one memorable piece in the style of Tom Wolfe before leaving for the Mirror to be replaced by Dalton, who was one of the most enterprising reporters I've ever known. He turned out well written copy day in and day out on just about any subject you could think of, from a borough council meeting to a miner killed in an accident to a woman umpire in a local league. Dalton and I once teamed up on an investigative story to ferret out corruption in the building of a new state police barracks. Turned out, the tip came from a stalwart Republican about a stalwart Democrat who was supposed to get the contract. There was no corruption but Dalton and I did figure out who Weinstein's anonymous—and erroneous—source was.

Two years after joining the CDT, we had a new building and a new press in College Township and my mood changed. Type was set much faster and I could process photographs easily. You could be more imaginative faster in page layout. I was also working on my master's degree in journalism a course at a time, although I had no clear idea why. I just sensed that the more degrees I had the better. It was a smart move. In 1975, after a year of teaching part

---

8 Dalton died in January 2017 after a long battle with Alzheimer's disease. After leaving the CDT in 1985, he taught at Castleton University in Vermont and then McDaniel College in Maryland from 1990-2012.

time, I joined the journalism faculty, a job I retired from in 2003. In the meantime, the Mirror and the CDT finally signed on for AP wirephoto. I remember them both boasting about it. It turned out to be a bonus for the editing course at Penn State. The instructors mined both newspapers for free photos to use in our classes. And the photographers at both newspapers got a break because they no longer had to come up with a photo a day for the front page.

On Dec. 31, 1977, the Mirror died and Centre County was no longer a two-newspaper town.

AHEAD OF ITS TIME – When man landed on the moon, the Pa. Mirror took advantage of its color printing press to publish a stunning front page. (Pa. Mirror photo)

CHAPTER 2
PAUL HOUCK AIMED FOR THE MOON

By James W. Houck

(Editor's note: Paul W. Houck was executive editor of the Pennsylvania Mirror from 1968 to 1976. His older son Jim is a retired Navy vice admiral, former law school dean, and member of the faculty at Penn State Law in University Park.)

In his heart of hearts, Paul Houck was a *newspaperman*. Not a journalist. Not a writer. Not a reporter, not even an editor. Though he did all those things over 30 years in the newspaper business, when it came right down to it, it was the finished whole – the newspaper itself – that he loved most. In his eyes, the daily newspaper was the booster engine of democracy. On a more personal level, the newspaper had been his friend and preoccupation from the day he got his first byline as a sophomore in high school. Even in the 60s, new newspapers were rare. So, it's little wonder that when he learned a new daily newspaper was about to launch in his

PAUL HOUCK ...
Newspaperman

native Centre County, he couldn't resist coming home to climb on board the rocket.

In addition to being a newspaperman, Paul Houck was my dad. As I came of age during the years 1968 to 1976, I watched him take off toward the moon, almost touch it, orbit around its dark side, and finally come hurtling back for a crash landing in the desert. These were eventful years for him and our family. This is how I remember our time with The Pennsylvania Mirror.

From Steel Valley to Happy Valley

In mid-1967, Dad's newspaper career was "all systems go." For a decade, he had been assistant to the publisher of the Homestead Daily Messenger, a daily paper located on the south bank of the Monongahela River in Pittsburgh's Mill District. Even though it published in the shadow of the larger and better-known Pittsburgh Press and Post-Gazette, the Messenger had established readership, solid advertising, and a respected presence in Pittsburgh's working-class suburbs. When my parents first learned that the paper was going to be sold, they fretted. But the new owners interviewed Dad, liked what they saw, and promoted him to the Messenger's top job. As a bonus, they made him general manager with complete day-to-day control over an additional five weekly newspapers spread across the Pittsburgh suburbs.

I was only nine at the time, but even then I had a sense that Dad was on a roll. We got a full-time company car, my parents started looking for a bigger house in a fancier neighborhood, and – most importantly – I was on track to get my own room. In later years, I found a folder stuffed with congratulatory letters from Pittsburgh civic leaders as well as newspaper industry luminaries. Life was good. Unbeknownst to me, however, his calculations were about to change.

In March 1968, Dad took a call from J.E. "Ted" Holtzinger, the venerable president of the Mirror Printing Company in Altoona. Mr. Holtzinger called to discuss his progress toward starting a new morning newspaper in State College and raised the possibility that Dad might come aboard. Dad had barely begun his new role managing six papers, but by late summer, the idea of clean, green, Happy Valley was looking good compared to the Steel Valley's "hot town summer in the city" vibe. Finally, on Aug. 5, 1968, Dad wrote to Blair Bice, the publisher of the new morning newspaper, expressing "interest in the new Central Pennsylvania paper." The letter made it official: Paul Houck was putting his hand up for the job of executive editor.

It made sense. Not many people knew the combination of central Pennsylvania and newspapers like he did. He had grown up in Bellefonte, just 5.5 miles northeast of the new paper's home office. At Bellefonte High School, he edited both the school newspaper and yearbook while finding time to deliver the Centre Daily Times on the side. His news carrier duties put him in touch with CDT staff member Jack Yeager, who recruited Dad as a sports stringer to collect Bellefonte-area box scores and game stats for transmission to the CDT's main office in State College.

Before long, they discovered the kid could write. Soon he was chasing fire bells and other news stories throughout Bellefonte, filling in for Yeager when the more experienced reporter had a bigger lead to chase. Often, after escorting his girlfriend home in time to satisfy her parents' curfew, Dad would head back downtown to get ink under his fingernails at the weekly Keystone Gazette's print shop. Newspapers were in his blood, and he hadn't even turned 18.

After a Navy enlistment that took him to the Pacific in 1944 and then post-war China, he returned to Centre County as a Penn State student, married Marilyn Shope (which ended her curfew), and soon was back on the beat as a full-time reporter for the CDT. He started in sports, moved to general news, and ended as the CDT's city editor. Over ten years, he learned the Centre Region as well as the local newspaper scene. He covered everything from the reopening of O.W. Houts' all-purpose store the day after it almost burned down, to Centre County's contribution to Truman's upset over Dewey, to the infamous 1953 prison riots at Rockview penitentiary. Along the way, he interviewed Penn State President Milton Eisenhower and his more famous brother, U.S. President Dwight Eisenhower. He met future President Ronald Reagan while he was in Centre County to do narration for a short film called "The Aaronsburg Story." And, in a harbinger of things to come, he knocked heads with his associate publisher and editor, who accused him of writing "loose leads" – too much creativity in the opening paragraphs of some of his stories. Dad pushed back, arguing that writing styles were changing, and he wanted to "stir the cobwebs."

In his August 1968 letter to Blair Bice, Dad made it clear that although he had left central Pennsylvania for Pittsburgh, he had been reading the Centre Daily Times steadily over the intervening 11 years and was "pretty well up on Central Pennsylvania affairs." He wrote that "from a professional standpoint, the CDT has to be considered one of the finest papers in Pennsylvania." However, he was optimistic about the challenge: "Even before I left, I knew it would be just a matter of time for the area to be ripe for another paper." He acknowledged that "creating the right image and a morning paper habit will not be as simple as pressing a button and turning out a beautiful paper. But it can be done with the proper ingredients and the proper hands at the wheels."

Soon, the deal was done. On Sept. 30, 1968, Dad became the first executive editor of the new Pennsylvania Mirror. He was 42.

Good Morning Central Pennsylvania!

On Dec. 11, 1968, the Mirror hit central Pennsylvania's front porches and newsstands. The front page sported a goofy cartoon of a human newspaper with a jolly keystone-shaped head proclaiming, "Good Morning Central Pennsylvania" in multicolor letters. "We have no traditions, no bad habits, and we can innovate our own innovations," Dad wrote in his first editorial. "Our goal . . . is to become great."

My goal was simpler: All I wanted to do was fit into my new neighborhood and school, and eventually I did. My middle and high school years (1969–1976) were happy and the Mirror was a positive drumbeat in the background. Probably more than most teenagers, my dad's job was part of my identity. For starters, I was a Mirror paperboy. I serviced my own route, delivered special editions all over town, and manned the Mirror's tent every summer at Grange Fair. But my identification with the Mirror went further. After all, when your dad's product shows up on doorsteps every day, people notice. I was proud that my friends, their parents, and even my teachers knew the Mirror. What does your father do? "He's the editor of the Pennsylvania Mirror!" "Oh right – good paper, I love the Mirror!" Or, "We can't afford two papers, but I enjoy their special editions." Or, "Great sports section - hey, who is T. Wes Brillik, anyway?"

I never tired of that last question! Who was Thaddeus Westmoreland Brillik? (Note how I use his full name to flaunt the depth of my Brillikian knowledge.) I'll rely on others to explain the man, the myth, and the legend, but suffice it to say, I did indeed know T. Wes. Brillik's true identity. Soon after T. Wes sent his first column from the top of Mount Nittany, Dad trusted me with the top-secret identity and threatened to waterboard me if I ever talked. Truth be told, I was more than happy to let my sports-page-reading friends know I *possessed* this valuable information. But, like Batman's butler Alfred, I never *revealed* the hero's identity. I sensed immediately that having the secret was more useful than spilling the beans, and I parlayed my insider status into the kind of cachet you can only get in high school. (If you doubt, check out page 293 of the 1976 State College Area High School Yearbook, where I allowed a friend to wear my custom-made Brillik t-shirt as compensation for appearing in the Mirror's yearbook sponsor ad.)

But I digress. As I got a little older, somewhere between high school sports injuries, I got serious about school and started reading beyond the Mirror's sports and comic pages. Back in pre-World Wide Web State College, the Mirror became my window into the

Vietnam War, campus protests, Nixon's visit to China, Watergate, and more. I began devouring the op-ed page and columns from the New York Times: the liberal James Reston, the humorist Russell Baker, and the incomparable language maven, William Safire. Safire's essays, along with his book, *Before the Fall*, chronicling his years as a Nixon speechwriter, were matches to my intellectual dry kindling. I wrote to Safire, asking for advice on how to become a great writer. His March 1975 response: "Read great novels – Melville and Mark Twain are best, and Joe Heller and Hemingway of the moderns, along with Robert Penn Warren. But above all, to be a great writer, write. If you don't like what you've written, the hell with it, write something else.") In the summer of 1975, Dad even cajoled Safire into spending 15 minutes with me in his Washington, D.C., office. I was star struck, and to this day have no idea what we talked about.

Suffice it to say that by the summer before my senior year in high school, I had developed my own interest in journalism. Looking back, this was probably inevitable. I was named after my dad's close friend, former CDT sports editor James Snyder, who died in a tragic auto accident in 1957, months before I was born. I spent (seemingly) whole years of my life between the ages of six and sixteen involuntarily assigned to an empty typewriter at a news desk on weekend afternoons while Dad wrapped up some project he promised, "will just take a few more minutes." Sitting still was hard, and I had free run of the Homestead Messenger's and later the Mirror's physical plants. The only rules were "don't bother the reporters while they're working" and "don't fall into the printing presses – I'll never be able to explain that to your mother." Through the years I learned all about darkrooms and teletypes, typeset and offset, bylines, cutlines, and deadlines. Kids that grow up in the military are known as "Army brats" or "Navy brats." I was a newspaper brat, and proud of it.

You might think my interest in my dad's business would have made him proud, but when it came time to start thinking about colleges, he kept steering me away from journalism programs and toward the U.S. Naval Academy in Annapolis, MD. He talked fondly of his time in the Navy and his pride in wearing the uniform. More pragmatically, he reminded me that in the difficult mid-70s economy, Naval Academy graduates had guaranteed jobs. "But I want to be a journalist," I protested. He said I should serve my country first. "Then, if you want, you can leave the Navy and go into journalism with some life experience under your belt. If you want to be in a business that holds institutions accountable, you should know what it's like to be inside one of those institutions first." That advice was sincere and logical. But it was also deft, because although I didn't know it at the time, he was doing his best to get me as far away from newspapers as possible. Across the country, newspapers were feeling the economic heat; at the Mirror, the heat shield was burning up.

This is a Spade . . . Call it That

Years would pass before I would learn how precarious the Mirror's financial position had been during the years 1968–1976. Barely a year after the Mirror's launch, an article written by a Penn State grad student in the January 1970 edition of *The Penn State Journalist* speculated about, "A New Newspaper's Struggle for Existence." That was premature. After all, when Ted Holtzinger founded the Mirror, he surely didn't expect a profit immediately. Five years later, however, he was running out of patience.

I am writing this during the corona virus quarantine, so I can't verify from external sources that the following piece actually ran, but Dad's draft for the Dec. 4, 1975, edition read as follows:

> Dame Rumor does not always check all the facts. We feel sure that many of our readers have heard rumors from time to time that this newspaper would be closed. . . . This time there is perhaps some truth to the rumor. We have just about exhausted the funds set aside to finance a new venture in first class journalism. Unless [we] can become self-supporting within the next six weeks, we shall be forced to suspend publication of a venture that started out with high enthusiasm on December 11, 1968.

> In that brief period of time we have won three first place sweepstakes awards for newspapers under 15,000 circulation, and one second place award. The awards were presented by the Pennsylvania Newspaper Publishers Association. The judges were outstanding journalists from states outside this state.
>
> We have also won national awards competing with newspapers from all the states. We have tried hard and the venture has been a success from all but a financial standpoint.

The last line seems akin to asking, "other than that, how was the play, Mrs. Lincoln?" But he had a point. By all accounts — including the passionate opinions expressed in numerous subscriber letters he received in the following weeks — the Mirror's content was strong.

Dad's announcement then proceeded to ask subscribers to give subscriptions as gifts and ask potential advertisers to purchase more advertising with the Mirror. Desperate as this may have been, apparently it helped, at least a bit. By Dec. 27, Dad was able to tell subscribers the Mirror had received a reprieve and would continue to operate.

But the glow didn't last. Back in those days, Dad had a plaque outside his office door consisting of a full-size shovel mounted above the words, "This is a Spade . . . Call it That." Sometime during those first months of 1976, I suspect the stress finally took its toll, and he apparently decided it was time to "call a spade a spade." He decided to tell management exactly what he thought. In the process, he may have dug his own grave.

Even then, I knew he had strong opinions about what ailed the Mirror. But it was only after he passed away that I found a copy of a 27-page, single-spaced, letter containing his painstaking (and painful) analysis of the problem. The letter was addressed to a member of the Mirror Printing Company board. I do not know if he ever sent it. I believe he did, but even if he didn't, I feel certain he conveyed the opinions some other way.

The letter contained a comprehensive and brutally frank discussion of the Mirror's problems, complete with an assessment of who should be held accountable for failings and what changes were needed not only in State College, but in Altoona as well. The letter went well beyond the scope of his official responsibility – as executive editor, he was responsible only for the paper's editorial content. However, his experience in the publishing business gave him the basis for an informed and broader critique. And critique he did. In an unsparing analysis of the current predicament, he believed the Mirror could prosper only if management would make key personnel changes; adopt a new streamlined management structure to exploit synergies between Altoona and State College operations; and create a fairer financial relationship with the subsidiary company (also owned by the Mirror Printing Company) that printed the Mirror. In short, he wanted to blow up the status quo.

At this point, the picture blurs. I don't know what happened, or who said what to whom. I was 17 and preoccupied with my final days of high school. What I do know is that not long after he wrote the letter, he was fired. And, inside two years, the Mirror was gone.

Through the years, I've wondered two things. First, if Dad's concerns had been addressed, would the Mirror have had a sustainable future? Second, even if the answer is yes, would it have mattered in the long run — would a solvent Mirror have survived the Internet revolution and fiscal tsunami that sunk so many newspapers in later years? I'm not qualified to answer either question. But I will confess to thinking that maybe, just maybe, the Mirror and its editor may have been ahead of their time.

In the 80s, after losing money for its first five years, the upstart paper USA Today began turning a profit. According to a 1987 Los Angeles Times article, up until that point, the belief had been that "there was just no way that a new newspaper — starting from scratch . . . could possibly succeed in the United States today." The article went on to note that after USA Today proved it was in for the long haul, even some respected newspaper editors had begun to praise "its pioneering use of color, its tight editing, its weather page, its sports statistics and its use of charts and graphs to help tell a story." The Times article continued, "Many papers have paid USA Today the ultimate compliment— they've copied it."

If many papers were copying USA Today in the 80s, it's only fair to point out that before there was USA Today, there was The Pennsylvania Mirror. Just a few months before that 1987 LA Times article, Dad had written me:

> There is some satisfaction, mixed with frustration, to see other newspapers now making a big thing over doing something the Mirror was doing 16-18 years ago.
>
> We were pace-setters, trail blazers putting out a new type of newspaper. Journalism schools, newspaper corporate offices, and newspaper operations departments accounted for anywhere up to 150 subscriptions a day. We were experimenting in black and white and color graphics, type styles, photo-toning, page makeups; it didn't matter that we were inconsistent in appearance. What was important was that we were consistently different. The staff understood that. The guys on the desk and on sports had a free hand in makeup; they knew I would not block something they wanted to try. They knew if it turned out lousy I'd probably have suggestions on improvements if they wanted to try it again. I had a lot of do's and don'ts that had to be taken as law, but that list did not include restrictions on experimenting with fresh ideas.
>
> But more than the appearance and the style of the product, the readers became comfortable with our integrity. We were not pompous. We kidded ourselves. We spoke firmly and clearly in our editorials. When necessary, we needled or kidded or slapped – and did so openly.

Ahead of its time or not, the Mirror was the last newspaper job my dad, the newspaperman, would ever have.

Perspective

Today, when we visit my parents' burial site, we drive north out of State College on PA Route 150, otherwise known as the Benner Pike. Three tenths of a mile past the old Shiloh Lutheran Church, we turn right to enter the cemetery. It's a peaceful place, suitable for reflection. But try as I might, it's hard to not notice the boxy, nondescript, brick building sitting directly across the street at 1015 Benner Pike. Yes, it's true: my parents are buried within line of sight from the Mirror's former home. Even in death, they couldn't quite get away. And yet, they chose their place of final repose voluntarily. Given how their Mirror years ended, one might wonder why.

Through the years, when I would tell Dad about something that was bothering me, he would inevitably say, "perspective, James, perspective. Never lose perspective." (I've always gone by "Jim," but when he went into "father mode," I became "James.") He meant, of course, that seemingly big things often aren't, and that black clouds have silver linings. In the 25 years after he left the Mirror, he and my mother found perspective. It didn't happen right away, but it came.

After crash landing in the desert with no rescue in sight, he wandered for two years, taking odd jobs here and there. He was trying hard but was essentially unemployed. Savings evaporated. Both his and my mother's parents were aging, my younger brother was approaching high school, and jobs for 50-year-old executive editors were hard to come by. Meanwhile, having gone off to Annapolis shortly after Dad was fired, I was rebelling. My grades were decent, but nearly every month I called home to harangue my parents about the bad decision I made

JIM HOUCK
… *Proud son*

going to Annapolis (and the implication they were responsible). I complained I wasn't meant to be in the Navy and the best thing for everyone would be for me to quit. But I didn't have the nerve. Instead, I whined. I made their worst years that much harder.

But eventually things turned around. In 1978, a good man named Roy Marlow came along and hired Dad at Penn State. For the next 13 years, they worked together in the Pennsylvania Technical Assistance Program (PENNTAP), a Penn State outreach service designed to assist small businesses. Dad did technical writing, marketing, and served as Marlow's de facto number two. It was a far cry from the responsibility of putting a newspaper on the street every day, but it had other advantages. He settled in. He worked more normal hours and found different ways to enjoy life and contribute. Even before he retired from the University in 1991, he and my mother socialized, traveled a little, doted on grandchildren, and celebrated over 50 years of marriage.

My younger brother, Tom (Thomas Paul Houck) is heir to Dad's appetite for creative, entrepreneurial challenges. In 1992, Tom quit a secure, executive-track job, and turned an original idea into an enduring multi-million-dollar business. In the beginning, when there was no one else, Dad provided moral support and lessons learned from the school of hard knocks, of which he was now a distinguished graduate. Most importantly, he helped develop messaging, marketing materials, and an innovative corporate newsletter that became a decade-long company staple. He was writing, and honing his late blooming talent for graphic illustration, until the end. Dad passed away in 2001, a month before the towers fell in New York.

And me? After turning in circles for two years at Annapolis, I buckled down, graduated, and embarked on a 32-year Navy career I can only describe as a blessing. But it wasn't preordained. Dad knew the military and I were a fit before I did. Fortunately, I trusted his judgment even when I didn't have his foresight.

The Houck family, and everyone else, moved on. But half a century later, I still wonder: Was the Mirror worth it? It's a fair question.

After all, the paper came and went in less than a decade. The CDT was before; the CDT was after. So, what exactly was the point?

I suspect everyone associated with "Central Pennsylvania's No. 1 Good Morning Paper" has at one time or another looked into their own mirror for an answer. The reflections will vary, but when I look for myself, the answer is clear.

The Mirror was an opportunity for my dad to take me into his world. (I didn't always want to be there, mind you, but he took me anyway.) Paul Houck lived, breathed, ate, and slept the Pennsylvania Mirror. To be around him was to do the same. Through countless conversations in car rides, over dinner, or recovering on the back porch after playing catch, he taught, and I absorbed, a seven-year tutorial on leadership. Years later, living in Florida with my own family, he and I added another chapter through our letter exchanges about the Mirror years. And after he died, I came upon the treasure of his dusty personal files, which allowed me to relive both his good and bad times through his own words.

What did I learn through my dad's experiences at the Mirror? I learned that leadership means breaking molds. I learned that leadership means being on the clock 24/7. I learned that big visions matter, but so does fine print. I learned that leadership is being accountable and making everyone around you accountable. I learned that leadership means having your peoples' backs, sometimes ferociously. I learned that leadership is often more about washing feet than it is standing tall. And I learned that leadership doesn't require yelling and screaming. At his funeral, someone said, "Your Dad was a gentleman." Nothing touched me more.

Above all, I learned integrity. Once, when I was 11 or 12, he was in a battle with somebody over something. I don't remember what it was, but I remember exactly where we were when we talked about it. We were driving past the Centre Furnace Mansion on East College Avenue, and I was worried. "Isn't it hard when important people don't like you?" His response: "It's a lot more important for people to respect you than it is for them to like you. Do your best, tell the truth, and treat people with respect. The rest takes care of itself." Yes, he said exactly that. I remember it like it was yesterday. He wasn't the first person to say some version of that, but he was the first person to say it so memorably to me. The Mirror years gave us that.

Was the Mirror worth it for him? Back to that spade: Seven years is a big investment only to see the enterprise fail. There were many tough days. Toughest of all was the night he told us he and the Mirror were done. I'll never forget the look on my mother's face. But there were great days too. The many Keystone Press Awards. The rapid reaction, widely circulated, "Flood of 72." The pioneering Sunday Mirror. The spirited fun of the "Back the Lions" campaign. The kind of dash and creativity that would lead a subscriber to say during "black December" '75:

> I know newspapers. I was at the Chronicle in San Francisco; the Post-Dispatch in St. Louis; and I worked against The Times in New York. I know you are about the finest newspaper I have ever read. The Mirror is very, very, good. The writing is tremendous. The flair for being different is marvelous. The freedom on your opinion page is so refreshing. I even read the sports pages. I care little about what is being written there, but I care a lot about how it is written and there cannot be any better sports writing anywhere. The whole paper is free and breezy. I can sense your staff love its work. I can sense honest journalism at its best.

And above all, there was the "moon issue."

Nothing made my dad prouder than The Pennsylvania Mirror's response to Neil Armstrong's epic walk. The Mirror's July 21st, 1969 banner headline grandly proclaimed: "Mankind approaches the universe." For Dad, however, the real headline was below the fold: "Readership of the Mirror today will exceed 110,000." The Mirror was given away free that day. I know, because I delivered it, tromping up and down College and Beaver Avenues and who knows how many side streets in the pre-dawn. He dragged me out of bed at 3 AM and I wasn't happy. But years later he told me:

> That single event helped propel the Mirror upward

in the minds of thousands of Central Pennsylvanians. We were on the street the next morning with half of page one showing a full color simulation. It registered in the minds of everyone as the real scene. Our phone rang off the hook that day asking for copies of the photo; newsstands ran out within minutes. . . . People were fascinated with history being made and we were giving it to them in the full color they couldn't get anywhere else.

Giving them what they "couldn't get anywhere else," was what the Mirror was all about. For me, the moon issue; especially that front page, represents the very best of those years. The lower right corner on page 1 contained a poem by Archibald MacLeish who wrote:

You were a wonder to us, unattainable, a longing past the reach of longing.

MacLeish was writing of the moon; for Dad, those words may as well have been written about the Mirror itself.

The Pennsylvania Mirror was Paul Houck's moon shot. He gave it his best. It didn't turn out the way he wanted, but all these years later, it hardly matters. He had a chance to fly, and he grabbed it. I'm so grateful I was there to watch.

CHAPTER 3
THE MAN WHO WAS THE CDT

By Thomazine Weinstein Shanahan

(Among my sources for this chapter are "Weinstein: His Life and Times" by T.L. Shaw in Town & Gown Magazine and "Former CDT editor Weinstein dies" by Barbara Brueggebors in the Centre Daily Times.)

Jerry Weinstein was a man of few words. He liked to tell his staff that any story could be told in six paragraphs. His right-hand man, Bill Welch, would say Jerry anticipated USA Today.

As my father, Jerry was my first and best writing teacher, so I acquired his preference for brevity. Years later, when I was in graduate school, I told him I'd been assigned to write a 50-page profile of a woman writer.

"How could anyone write 50 pages?" he asked, seriously.

On the other hand, as editor of the Centre Daily Times from 1945 to 1980, he estimated that he'd written more than 10,000 editorials. Writing them became his passion. They were brief, of course, and were almost always about Centre County matters.

In looking back over his career he observed that his and the paper's

*PROUD DAUGHTER –
Thomazine Weinstein Shanahan reveals the personal side of her father. (R. Thomas Berner photo)*

accomplishments included open meetings by local government bodies, merging of schools into jointures, new property evaluations, and equalization of county assessments. Frank to acknowledge the losses, he named the failure to save a section of the Willowbank building for a Bellefonte medical facility, and not foreseeing the extent of destruction that building the State College bypass would bring to Oak Hall.

Born in Meyersdale, Pa., on Aug. 28, 1916, Jerry moved with his family to Brooklyn while in grade school. He loved to tell people that he graduated from Manual Training High School in Prospect Park. He chose it because it was the only school with a swimming pool.

He had begun swimming at the New York Athletic Club when he was 12, and was recruited there by Manual Training. Swimming became one of his lifelong loves; the other was writing for newspapers.

His first writing job was as a stringer for the New York World Telegram where he covered high school sports. It didn't pay much— probably 5 cents an inch—and he asked for a raise. When the editor turned him down, Jerry asked why. He said he was as good as anyone else in the newsroom and asked what they had that he didn't.

The answer: a college degree.

That September in 1934 he arrived at the Bellefonte train station with $300 he had borrowed from his brother and began his student life at Penn State. My father loved to tell my sister, Judy, and me how he worked his way through college. He was a lifeguard at the Glennland pool, a paid Collegian staffer, and an assistant to Ridge Riley in the University's sports information department.

And he swam—on Penn State's first swimming team.

He became sports editor of the CDT on April 1, 1937, a year before he graduated with a journalism degree. While working at the paper, he met Jack Yeager, who was associate editor covering Bellefonte and the courts. Jack was married to Liza Curtin, daughter of H.L. Curtin, the last iron master of the Eagle Iron Works at Curtin, north of Bellefonte. Many evenings Jack would take Jerry to Curtin to spend an evening with his father-in-law. The three men would be visiting and at some point my mother, Thomazine,[9] then in high school, would come home from a date and go in to say good night.

Later, when my father decided to go to Philadelphia to work for the AP, he mentioned that to my grandmother, who told him that Thommy was about to begin nursing school there. She said, "Please take care of Thommy."

He did. He married her. In fact, they eloped, and were married by a justice of the peace in Elkins Park, Pa. He worked for the AP and she finished her degree in nursing.

World War II intervened, and Jerry spent 37 months in the U.S. Army Air Corps, serving first as a drill instructor and later as the editor of a 100,000 circulation service newspaper distributed throughout the Caribbean area. Jerry and Thommy lived in Miami Beach, where a daughter (me) and son were born.[10] His staff at the paper included a first-rate photographer and a talented cartoonist. As a result, I have hundreds of baby pictures taken from the day of my birth until we left Florida in 1945. And of course my birth announcement and my brother's were in the form of splendid cartoons (try to describe).

After the war, my parents intended to return to Philadelphia where he would continue writing for the AP. Gene Reilly had other ideas. He was running the CDT with no staff and he wanted my father to help him out. My father recalled "I sat for a few minutes and thought where I'd like to live and work, but mainly where I'd like to raise a family. It didn't take long to decide on State College. I became editor and Gene became business manager." The boy from Brooklyn became a small-town guy.

The town filled up as G.I.s arrived to get their college degrees and housing was scarce. My parents, with two small children, lived with my mother's family in the ironmaster's mansion at Curtin. It was a big house but a crowded one. My grandmother, my parents and two children, my Uncle Bud with Aunt Liz and their three children, my Uncles George and Jim, both bachelors, all lived there.

---

9 My mother and I were both named Thomazine, a popular name for women in the Curtin family. My mother was known as Thommy and I as Timmy. My mother was the fifth and I the sixth Thomazine. My daughter Tina is the 7th.

10 My brother Michael died when he was 3. Eventually, my parents had another daughter, Judy, who is six years younger than I.

My father had no car, so publisher Claude Aikens lent him an old station wagon, the kind with wooden panels, so he could make the 17-mile trip to town. Each morning he would get up before daybreak. As he left the house he was greeted by George and Jim, coming in after a night on the town.

"Good morning, Jerry," they'd say.

"Goodnight, boys," Jerry replied.

My father had a reputation for his sardonic wit. Tom Berner, who was the city editor for four years, recalls that when he first met my father at an editors' conference in 1971, my father asked him, a recent college graduate, what he was going to do.

"I'm going to grad school," Berner replied.

"Why," my father asked.

"To stimulate my mind," Berner believes he replied.

My father guffawed and said: "You can do that with drugs."

From the beginning of his time as editor, Jerry's focus was on service to the public. "The readers—that's what mattered most to Jerry, and that's what made him a great editor," said former Times staffer Paul Poorman.[11]

"For him, the newspaper was a very important tradition in the county. He taught me that I shouldn't just write for the University professors, but also for the farmers and miners in the outlying areas," said his niece, the former Molly Yeager.

The public included everyone who lived in Centre County. When occasional readers complained that they wanted to see more national stories in the paper, Jerry told them they could get that anywhere. "Your kid scored a goal last night. Go clip the story about that out of the [Philadelphia] Inquirer."

"Jerry's devotion to the county led him to make sure that everyone in the news department had a part in covering community news," John Brutzman, a former staffer, said. "We were all known somewhere in

---

11 Poorman followed his job at the CDT with jobs at the Harrisburg Patriot, the Philadelphia Bulletin, the Detroit News and the Akron Beacon-Journal. He also taught at Northwestern and finished his career as a lobbyist for Kent State University. He was 61 when he died in 1992. My father was always delighted when someone who started at the CDT moved up bigger jobs.

the community, and weren't just faceless journalists hiding behind bylines." Besides assigning staff to local stories, Jerry himself took part in community activities. He fought for open meetings, saying, "We got the Penn State board of trustees to open a meeting right before the sunshine laws were passed. We also opened the courthouse."

So strongly did he feel about open meetings he ran for a place on the Centre County Hospital board of trustees, was elected, and served for two and a half years. In 1955 he resigned because a Bellefonte newspaper wasn't allowed in a meeting.

"I think we did a lot for students and education," Jerry said, "by writing quite a few editorials. I got some strong calls from Governor Shafer, both commending me and giving me hell. But we always criticized the University constructively."

That constructive criticism led to a project working with the University's journalism and English departments' intern programs. Philip Klass, former director of the English department's intern program, once wrote, "Jerry helped put together much of the program well before internships had become acceptable to most departments in the humanities, and, in his Friday afternoon sessions, he growled and glowered creative writing students into an understanding of how they could express themselves and yet do the world's daily work."

One of his best editorial ideas was the popular Good Evening column, which appeared on page one. It began in the 1950s as a place where readers could request help for needy people or organizations, suggest solutions for community problems or submit stories that didn't fit anywhere else.

Soon, though, Good Evening expanded to include news of the sighting of the first robin or green tomato, wise sayings of children, comments on unusual weather. Readers loved it and enjoyed sending in their own stories. There was a running joke in our family that any story or anecdote in the household was likely to turn up in slightly disguised form in Good Evening.

Berner admits that some people found the column corny but he delighted in the irony of a phone call he got one day from someone who wanted something in the "trivia column." Berner recalls that the column became so popular listing lost and found items, that my father created a free classified ad section labeled "Good Evening Classifieds."

My father took pride in guiding the Centre Daily Times from a six-page daily into a respected regional institution. In 1979 the paper was sold to Knight-Ridder for $15.5 million. Retiring in 1980, Jerry's life took a whole new turn.

He and my mother spent winters in Florida, near Harold and Irma Zipser, also of State College. The warm weather helped his arthritis and they both played golf and swam. Jerry devoted their springs and summers in State College to his other love, swimming. He swam 40 minutes a day at the Natatorium at Penn State, and taught classes for those with physical limitations. He especially enjoyed helping people who were afraid of water to become comfortable in it.

Retired Penn State Aquatic Director, Armand "Buzz" Shaner, said "He's devoted to the water, and knows he's benefited from it. He gives to others in the same way."

By December 1989 my father's health was deteriorating. He had long struggled with rheumatoid arthritis and emphysema. My mother admitted that life was becoming more difficult by the day. Except for his swimming he rarely left the house and he saw almost no one. She said, "If only he could find something he enjoys doing."

I thought about my father and how restricted his life had become since his retirement as editor. He, who had written at least six editorials a week for nearly forty years, now wrote only the occasional letter on his battered typewriter on which he typed using only two fingers, a method referred to as "hunt and peck" typing.

In that week between Christmas and New Year's I wrote him a letter. My hope was to get him writing again and I thought I'd come up with an idea that might tempt him. I told him that I felt the story of his marriage to my mother—how it came about and how they lived it out—would be a great gift to us, his family, and probably of interest to many.

After all, in 1942, few Jewish men from Brooklyn met and married the blonde daughter of an old WASP family in central Pennsylvania.

How they met, how their families and friends reacted, how they created a good life together—surely this was raw material for a good tale.

I ended the letter "If you write just one page a day, in a year you'll have a book." I mailed the letter from Washington and hoped he would get it by the New Year.

Deep in the night of Jan. 2 my mother called to say my father had suffered a major heart attack and was in intensive care. By daybreak we were on the road to State College—my sister and her two small children, and my 20-year-old daughter. We got there in time to see him. He lived for 10 days, conscious and communicative, but was finally unable to breathe on his own.

My father died on Jan. 12, 1990, at Centre Community Hospital He was 73.

He had always told us he did not want a funeral, only to be buried with the Curtins in Union Cemetery in Bellefonte. Jewish by birth, he was never observant and encouraged my mother, my sister, and me to attend the Episcopal Church. We felt there needed to be some public event to honor his life. Back in 1990, the practice of holding celebrations of life was rare.

James Trost, rector of St. Andrew's Episcopal church, became a close friend of my father, and of mine, and I suggested to Jim that I ask Rabbi Jeffrey Eisenstat of Congregation Brit Shalom, to meet with us and plan a service. Jeff graciously agreed, and the three of us sat down with the Hebrew Bible, the Christian Bible, and a hymnal. The resulting service seemed to please Jewish and Christian friends and family. For my 7-year old nephew, Thomas Jerome Bergan, the sight of Joe Paterno among the guests was a highlight of his young life.

In the days immediately following his death, my mother asked if I'd gotten a letter from him after the Christmas visit. No, sadly, I had not. She said she was almost certain he'd been writing one, that he had loved the idea of writing a memoir. She kept looking through his immaculately organized maple desk, and eventually came up with an 8- by 10-inch sheet of yellow note paper.

On it he had listed 15 topics:

Weinstein pronunciation — ine in New York, een in New Jersey.

After-school jobs
Pre-1929 vacation homes
Russia Germany theories[12]
Aunt Jenny
MTHS – Manual Training High School
Journalism 5 cents an inch
Friends
Prejudice
1937 CDT—Yeager and Curtin
PSU work, study, graduation
Swim to job to Gal—Rutgers-PSU
Religious background
CDT – AP
Army (work!) Escape Korea
Post WWII Housing

How I wish I could have talked to him about these tantalizing bits and pieces. Even more, how I wish I could have read what he might have written.

GOOD TEAM – Jerry Weinstein and his wife, Thomazine, kneeling on left in front row, blended in with a strong Centre Daily Times newsroom staff in this 1950s photo. (Photo courtesy of the CDT)

---

12 I have no idea what that refers to. Weinstein is a Judeo-German name. Perhaps some ancestor of my father's was Russian and he wanted to write about it.

CHAPTER 4
WHO ARE THOSE GUYS?

By Ron Bracken

There's a scene in the movie Butch Cassidy and the Sundance Kid where the two of them are lying atop a ridge watching a posse of Pinkerton detectives relentlessly pursuing them across the valley floor far below. One looks at the other and says, "Who are those guys?"

In the late fall of 1968 when the Pennsylvania Mirror was launched, that's how those of us at the staid Centre Daily Times viewed the sports staff at the Mirror.

DOUBLE COVERAGE – Ron Bracken, left, and Terry Nau interview Matt Suhey during 1976 Penn State Media Day. (Pa. Mirror photo)

Who were those guys? They could have been the Delta Tau Chi fraternity in Animal House. They were irreverent, anti-establishment but, unlike Bluto Blutarski and his brothers, they were talented as hell. They might have had the greatest collection of sportswriters in the history of Centre County.

They wore t-shirts to events while we at the CDT wore shirts and ties. You could not have found two more opposite staffs. And that made it fun to cover sports in the county from 1968 through 1977. Because whatever competition we were covering, the competition between the Mirror and the CDT was just as intense.

***

Call me the Accidental Sportswriter.

When I walked onto the sidelines at Hilltop Stadium in Houtzdale in September of 1967 to cover the BEA-Moshannon Valley football game it was my first venture into the world of sports writing, or writing of any kind. I was greener than the grass on the field that night.

I've always been a believer in fate. There's no other way to explain how I wound up carrying a clipboard at that game.

Bear with me while I tell you that story. In the summer of 1967 I was working for Penns Valley Publishing, a small company which recodified borough ordinances. There cannot possibly be a more boring way to earn a paycheck than rewriting an archaic ordinance from the town of Perkasie. But I was married and a new father and needed a job. The company rented office space in the back of the Centre Daily Times building at 119 S. Fraser St. in downtown State College.

Because I was playing baseball in the Centre County League at the time I would bring the box score to work with me in the morning and hand deliver it to Times Sports Editor Doug McDonald rather than calling it in the night of the game. At the end of the summer, when I gave Doug our last box score, just on a whim, I asked him if he needed any help covering high school football that

DURABLE –
Ron Bracken still contributes sports articles to the CDT.

fall. Understand, I had never even taken a journalism course in my two years at Penn State, although I got an A in English 1.

Doug said that as a matter of fact, he did. One of the stringers he had covering high school football was leaving two weeks into the season and if I wanted I could tag along with the guy and watch what he did, then come back to the office and write a game story. As I said, I was green so I went back to the office, sat down and wrote the story longhand, then typed it.

Doug read it and said it was acceptable, but there was no way I could take the time to write a story longhand and then type it. If I could type it without the detour I could have the job. Which is how I wound up in Houtzdale that night.

When the next day's CDT came out, I couldn't wait to open it and see my byline. I still have the clipping of that story.

On Monday morning, I was at my desk deep into Perkasie's ordinances. Times editor Jerome Weinstein appeared in the doorway and beckoned me to come into the hall. I figured it was to tell me my newspaper career was over. Instead he said he liked the story and offered me a job in the sports department which, at that time, consisted of Doug.

I declined. I knew the newspaper business was all about working nights and weekends and I didn't want that with a newborn at home. But as the season went along I became more and more enamored of the job. I loved being on the sideline on a Friday night with the smell of burning leaves and the whole atmosphere surrounding a high school football game.

So on a Sunday night after the season ended, my wife and I were watching the Smothers Brothers on television, and I told her I was going in to the CDT office the next morning to see if that job was still available, that I didn't want to get 10 years down the road and wish I had taken it.

The next morning I knocked on Weinstein's door and asked about the job. He told me someone was coming in to interview for it at noon that day.

As fate would have it, the guy didn't show up, the job was mine and the rest is, well, you know.

***

It was a classic case of taking a knife to a gun fight, me being the guy with the knife in my hand.

There was no way in the world I was prepared to get into a writing contest with the sports staff of the Pennsylvania Mirror.

They were talented, educated, experienced. When I started at the CDT, I was a fan with a clipboard and a love of sports going back to when I was 12 and bought a Milwaukee Braves stamp book at the Clover Farm store for a quarter. Actually, I was hooked long before that when my father and a friend took me to Pittsburgh to see the Pirates play the New York Giants in a Sunday doubleheader. We had seats in the left field bleachers, and by the time the second game rolled around I was ready to go home. That would have been in the early '50s when the Pirates were terrible. But I liked them and could recite their entire starting lineup. It was only later that I became the lone Braves fan in Port Matilda.

I was always a Penn State fan. It took years in the newspaper business to beat that out of me. Hell, in the fall of 1967, a friend of mine and I got jobs as ushers in Beaver Stadium just to see the games. The next year I was in the press box when Penn State opened the season with Navy. That's when I began interacting with the guys from the Mirror. And wondering who those guys were. Over the course of the next nine years there were plenty of interactions, some of which were truly memorable, as you will see.

In 1975, the PIAA wrestling championships were held in Penn State's Rec Hall. By then I was a full-blown ink-stained wretch, loving every minute of it. The press seating for the tournament was on the track that circled the gym. Fans were right in front of us, well within our reach, which cost one young fan his beloved Cincinnati Reds batting helmet. As it turned out, the helmet belonged to the son of a neighboring newspaper's sports editor. Didn't matter. For some reason that helmet drew Terry Nau's ire, so he reached over the railing and took a fist to the top of the helmet, causing it to split right down the middle.

Later, as the crowd filtered in for the finals after spending the break at the various downtown bars and restaurants, the photographers ringed the mat, stretched out on the floor. And there was Nau among them. Apparently he didn't blend in well, because I. Charles McCullough, the PIAA executive director and a large man, tapped Nau on the shoulder and asked him who he was.

"Would you believe...Doug McDonald?" Nau said.

You could not have had two more different individuals than Terry and Doug, one an irreverent Vietnam vet, the other a saintly scribe. And McCullough knew Doug well from years of dealing with him. He was not impressed with Nau's answer. I don't recall if he kicked Nau out of the event or just told him to get up on press row.

In the Mirror's sunset years Chance B. Conner joined its staff. Chance was a State College High graduate who had played baseball for the Little Lions. So he was the natural choice to cover the Centre County Baseball League playoffs. Made up of teams from the small towns in the County, the playoffs were serious stuff. Not necessarily so to Conner, who may or may not have had a few adult beverages before he arrived at Howard for the game with Port Matilda, two bitter rivals. There is no preferred seating for the media at these games. You showed up, got the lineups and then found a spot where you could watch the game.

Having arrived late, Conner wound up far down the right field line. Midway through the game a Port batter hit a foul ball down the right field line which Conner fielded. No one noticed the small delay before he threw the ball back in to the umpire who put it in the ball bag he carried. Later there was another foul ball out of play and the umpire reached into the ball bag, grabbed a ball and threw it in to the pitcher.

As the pitcher began rubbing up the ball he could be heard saying "What the hell?" What had caught his attention was the writing on the ball. "Chance B. Conner." Yep, the Mirror representative had autographed the foul ball before he threw it back to the umpire an inning earlier.

Unthinkable. Irreverent. Unacceptable to such an institution as the County League. Funny as hell too.

That's what made the Mirror staff fun to be around. You never knew what might happen, whose nose they might tweak. No one was better at that than the late Dennis Gildea, whose alter ego was none other than T. Wes Brillik. One of Brillik's great joys in life, outside of drinking Utica Club beer, was to poke fun at the sports establishment in Centre County. Read that Penn State and State College High School or the Nits and the Little Nits as he called them

Each week during football season he wrote a prediction column in which he always picked the Big Nits and Little Nits to lose regardless of who they were playing. And he was outrageously rude to both. He once said the Little Lion cheerleaders were ugly as swamp creatures in a Disney movie.

Once he picked Penns Valley to beat Curwensville, a team he described as "the worst eleven in the state." That triggered a flood of telephone calls to the editor from furious Curwensville residents.

At the CDT, we, like a lot of readers, couldn't wait to see what Brillik had to say. Even today I still have people asking me when Brillik is coming back. He had a cult following. The mainstream, stiff-necked county readers despised him and said he should have been fired. What a waste of talent that would have been.

Later Gildea came over to the dark side and joined the CDT staff when the Mirror folded. While there he pulled a great prank on me.

In 1985, Penn State was set to play Oklahoma in the Orange Bowl in a game that would decide the national championship. But we had a problem at the CDT. Sports editor Jim Carlson's wife was due to have their first child at about the same time as the game and he was not about to leave her alone while he went to Florida. The plan was for Carlson and me to cover the game so now we had a staffing problem.

Around the office I had the reputation as a practical joker, but Gildea got me good once. He teamed up with managing editor Karen Lobeck and hatched a plot that there would be a young news reporter to join me at the Orange Bowl, who was to cover the game from a news angle. Early one afternoon Lobeck called me into her office and told me who my travel companion was going to be—the young reporter was a good looking, single brunette woman—and announced that the CDT was only willing to pay for one hotel room.

"That's not going to work,' I croaked. "No way."

I didn't know that Gildea was standing outside the window of Lobeck's office taking immense pleasure at my obvious discomfort. Finally, Lobeck couldn't stick to the plan any longer and told me Gildea would actually be the one accompanying me to Miami. He was disappointed that the plan didn't hold together a little longer. Actually, it did. When I got home, I told my wife what was being planned, and I was right when I told Lobeck there was no way that plan would work, at least not if I wanted to remain married.

My last experience with the Mirror was in December of 1977 at the Fiesta Bowl.

It was Penn State's first trip to the Arizona-based bowl and in those days it was still played on Christmas Day.

The CDT had sent me to the game, and the Mirror had dispatched Conner. By this time we had become friendly adversaries and were comfortable around each other. During the week leading up to the game there were daily press conferences, and I would see Chance at those.

Then one day he wasn't there. I just figured he had been enjoying the desert night life and thought nothing more of it. But he was gone the next day as well. That night when I filed my stories, I talked to whoever was manning the desk at the CDT, and he told me the Mirror had folded, which explained Conner's absence. He had no paper for which to write.

And unlike Butch and Sundance, I really missed those guys.

CHAPTER 5
WORK HARD, PLAY HARD!

By Terry Nau

(EDITOR'S NOTE: Terry Nau served as sports editor of the Pennsylvania Mirror from 1972-77.)

When I joined the Pennsylvania Mirror's staff after graduating from Penn State in March 1972, I fell in with a group of scribes who could write creatively and party hard after deadline. As a collegiate sportswriter, I polished those same skills, so my transition into the working world went smoothly.

My boss at the Mirror, a red-haired Irishman named Dave Fay, bumped into me for the first time at the Shandygaff Saloon a year earlier. When I picked up his beer by mistake and drained it, Fay smiled and ordered another for both of us. (Glasses of beer cost a quarter in those days.) It was the beginning of an erratic friendship fueled by alcohol and perceived slights. Dave was Old School, did not go to college, went to the Navy instead, and liked to say of reporters after editing their stories, "You can send them to school, buy 'em books, but you can't

TERRY NAU
... *A few regrets*

teach 'em common sense." A Navy veteran, Dave tolerated me because I had been drafted into the Army before college and spent time in Southeast Asia. I also had red hair and could easily have passed for Dave's younger brother.

I met Dennis Gildea, a Villanova graduate who grew up in the dusty town of Coaldale, during my first month at Penn State, back in September 1970, when we both covered PSU soccer games for our respective newspapers. I was still a student, writing for the Daily Collegian, and Dennis was into his second year as a sportswriter for the Mirror. We traveled to road games together and struck up a friendship that would last for nearly 50 years.

Rounding out the sports staff was John Andrews, who split his time between designing pages and writing gymnastics stories. He was a quiet fellow in his mid-30s from a small town outside of Harrisburg called Duncannon. A few years older than us, "J.D.," as he was known in his bylined stories, had worked at the Wall Street Journal in the 1960s, fleeing New York City, he said, after waking up one morning to find a cockroach sitting on top of his toothbrush.

Nicknamed "Beaver," for reasons unknown to me, John returned to his alma mater, Penn State, and took a job at the Mirror shortly after it launched in 1968. He only cared to report on Penn State gymnastics and its legendary coach, Gene Wettstone. The words came slowly from Beaver's typewriter, but they fit together into fascinating stories about a complex sport most of us had only seen on television during the Summer Olympics.

Dave Fay decided I should lead this three-person staff. Beaver was the likely choice but did not want to work full-time. That was his excuse, even though his so-called short weeks often ran over 40 hours, and by 1977 he was up to 60 hours. None of us cared about money in those days. I made around $120 per week, and sometimes earned overtime wages. In football season, I would often work 60 hours a week (with maybe three hours of overtime pay).

Saturdays were crazy days. Penn State's press box opened at 11 a.m., the game ended around 4, interviews lasted for an hour, and then came five more hours in the office, writing several stories for our midnight deadline. Around 10 or 11 at night, leaving Beaver to finish the pages, Dennis and I would bolt downtown

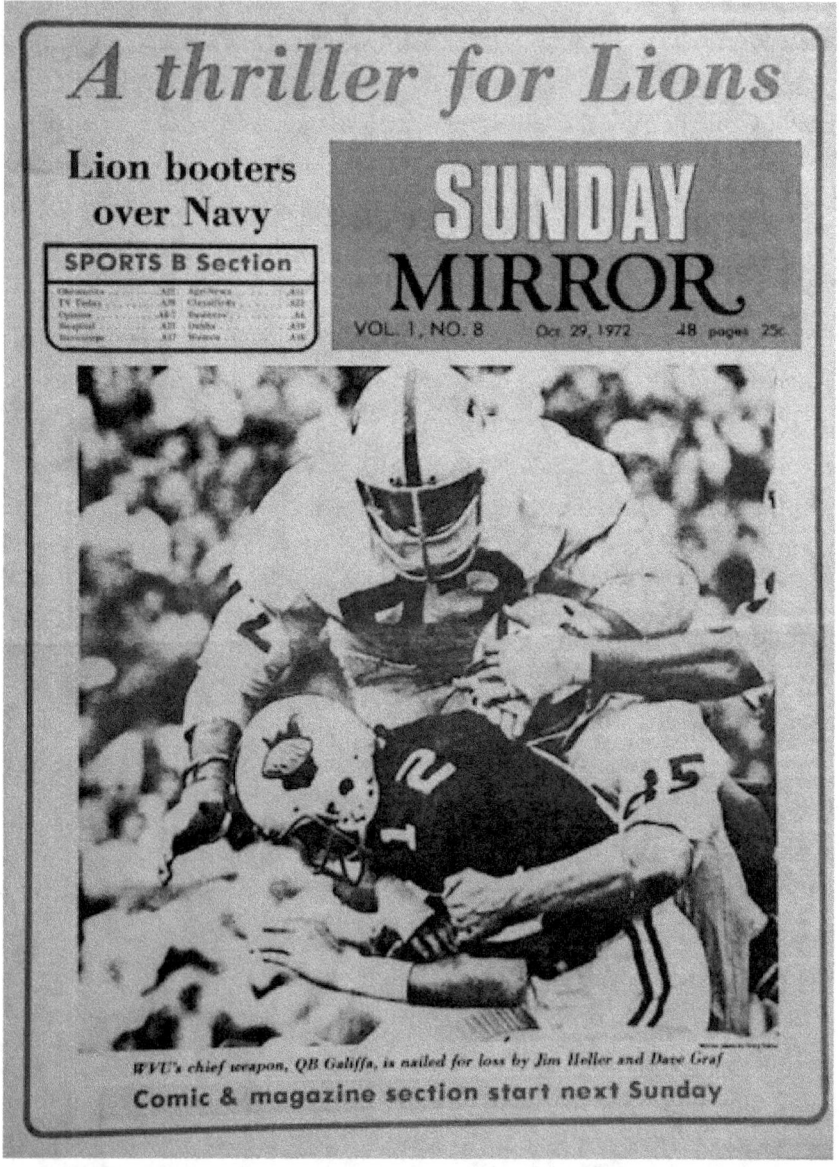

GOING BIG – Executive editor Paul Houck created a 48-page Sunday Mirror section filled with 24 pages of sports. (Greg Guise photo)

for several quick beers and return in time to watch our product roll off the printing press at 2 in the morning. Seeing our work so quickly turned into print was such a satisfying feeling! We exulted over photographs and stories, and groaned over the mistakes we made in the rush to deadline. We were young and excited about our profession.

When football season rolled around in September 1972, the Mirror's executive editor, Paul Houck, boldly launched a 48-page Sunday tabloid with 24 pages devoted to sports. The Mirror would bring results of Saturday's Penn State football game to readers 30 hours before our competition, the Centre Daily Times, hit the streets on Monday afternoon. And since we had 24 pages to fill, a lot of national college football game stories got into our Sunday section along with NFL news and major league baseball coverage.

The CDT reached 18,000 households six days a week, approximately twice the Mirror's circulation ... except for Sundays during football season when the Mirror was the only game in town. Our Sunday section sold enough ads to earn a profit in that first year, but it was only one day out of the week. The daily Mirror sports section often featured six wide-open pages with only a few ads. We piled a huge amount of national sports news into the section, including major league baseball box scores, something rarely seen in smaller newspapers of the day. We built a small "cult" following of sports-oriented readers.

My leadership skills were seriously challenged at the Mirror, where I worked with two older sportswriters. This was different than my college experience, or the Army where at age 20 I headed a 10-man artillery section of soldiers mostly my own age. As sports editor of the Collegian, I assigned stories to eager students three years younger who may have been intimidated by my cranky office temperament.

At the Mirror, I had little sway over work schedules. Dennis usually arrived late in the afternoon, and Beaver not far behind him. That first summer, central Pennsylvania was hit by two weeks of rain (aka Hurricane Agnes). The storm canceled all outdoor sports events and sent rivers flowing over their boundaries. One of our downtown friends, Pat Daugherty, was activated by the National Guard and dispatched to Wilkes-Barre where coffins sprung from their graves were floating in the streets. Pat helped put the skeletons back into the coffins. He told that story to great effect at the Tavern Restaurant, where he first worked as a waiter and eventually bought the place in the 1980s with his friend, Bill Tucker.

During this lengthy storm, we had to invent sports stories every day while trying to fill six pages with local copy and national sports news. I usually went on campus during the day to search for a story or two. Dennis would arrive at the office in late afternoon, often with nothing to write about, wearing a green visor over his head as he set up shop in the empty office of the women's page editor, who worked the day shift. I would ask him what he might be writing about. Shrug of the shoulders.

"I only write when I have something to say," he told me.

Finally yielding to my desperate pleas, Dennis magically invented his alter ego, T. Wes Brillik, who lived on top of Mount Nittany with his girlfriend, Mimsy. Brillik could write in any kind of weather. His prose flowed in a Gaelic-like frenzy, creating characters based on satirical renditions of public figures, some obscure, others rather well-known. Brillik's weekly stories began to gain favor inside our quirky Mirrow (Brillik's spelling) readership, which featured a litany of college professors, rugged outdoorsmen, and college students killing time between classes.

The public wanted more of Brillik. We made T. Wes an unpaid member of the sports staff and he soon got under the skin of local fans and coaches as he picked the home teams to lose every week. People called the office, asking for the real name of this Brillik fellow. It was suggested even Joe Paterno wanted to know. We never revealed the secret, although it seemed fairly obvious to me that Dennis was the only writer on our staff capable of inventing something so creative.

My only route to survival as sports editor was to let Dennis and Beaver have their personal freedom. I was just minding the store while covering the major Penn State beats those two did not want to get involved in. Beaver had season tickets to Nit football games. He expressed no interest in joining the media swell that covered the program, preferring to sit in the stands with his wife, Jane, and friends from Duncannon and cheer the home team on. Then he would come to work and design a complete sports section for our Sunday paper, leaving the office only after the paper had rolled off the printing press. His wife, often called "Chain" by her husband, worked for free on Friday nights and weekends, editing stories as they came out of our typewriters. Jane was a great copy editor. She even wrote a few gymnastics stories when a big meet came along.

John Andrews was the heart and soul of our sports staff from the first day I sat down at the editor's desk. He was a stickler for details, the copy editor we all needed. And Jane never let a gram-

SPORTS EDITORS – Jane Andrews often donated her time on busy nights to edit copy while her husband John designed the pages. John died in 2017 but Jane lives on. (Dave Hamilton photo)

matical error slip past her eye, turning stories back to us even as her husband pleaded for copy.

Dennis preferred what he called "Third World" sports — soccer, cross-country, track, tennis, and wrestling. So we complemented each other, the three of us. I would do desk (designing the pages) early in the week and Beaver would handle the busy Friday and Saturday shifts, freeing me to tackle the growing octopus that was Penn State football. We certainly didn't cover the local high school scene as thoroughly as the CDT did, owing to our midnight deadline, but again we had the morning/afternoon advantage.

With most every Penn State "minor" sport covered, that left me with football, basketball and baseball. Right up my alley. My job was not without benefits. Over my five-plus years at the Mirror, I flew to bowl games in New Orleans and Dallas, and made road trips to Colorado and San Francisco, all on the Mirror's dime. One Saturday morning, I jumped into a two-seat airplane with local pilot Jim Ascah at the helm, and flew to West Point for a 1 p.m. kickoff, returning in time to file my game story for the midnight deadline. The plane ride over the mountains was more fun than a chopper flight in Vietnam.

Covering Penn State football involved a lot of time and energy. My writing style leaned more towards quantity over quality because we had pages to fill. The Mirror's lack of advertising put a lot of pressure on us to fill space. We could write as many words as we wanted, as long as we wrote fast and with an attitude. Nobody told us what to write, or complained about negative stories. "Just don't get us sued," might have been our one rule. The Mirror was a sportswriter's paradise.

Joe Paterno never let a negative paragraph get past him. Not that he read newspapers first thing in the morning. He had (sports information directors) Jim Tarman and John Morris do that, and then relay to him any offending passages. This was never a big deal to me because criticism is part of any newsman's job. You learn from mistakes and stick up for your beliefs. Besides, Joe was fun to cover. The city slicker from Brooklyn quoted Shakespeare and envisioned his football program as "The Grand Experiment," where players actually went to class, and sometimes took exams on the morning of games, as Sports Illustrated revealed in a 1969 story about All-America linebacker Dennis Onkotz. I had many positive stories to write, too.

And yet, my journalistic instincts often took me to the dark side. Over the years, I have reflected on this because I am generally positive about life, but maybe I was transferring the anti-everything attitude spawned by the Vietnam War and so common during the tumultuous 1970s. I knew who the unhappy players in the locker room were and sometimes heard them out, usually in a bar downtown. If they had a legitimate beef, their stories might find a spot in the Mirror. I was 25 years old and enjoyed challenging authority. Paterno's football program already had a lofty opinion of itself and I sought to stick a pin in that balloon whenever possible.

Ron Bracken was the CDT writer I went up against most often. A talented writer, still in his 20s, just learning his craft (as we all were), Ron would become a friendly rival. He grew up in nearby Port Matilda and killed us on high school sports coverage. But we could gain an advantage with our irreverent Penn State perspective – and the unchallenged Sunday edition. That attitude extended into everything the Mirror crew wrote about Penn State. Gildea turned our normally dull weekly football prognostications column into a controversial undertaking. Under his own byline, Dennis would frequently pick against the Nits. And then he would write a Brillik column that always went for the other team. I would pick against Penn State when they faced legitimate opponents (which only happened two of three times a season). In 1973, we both went against unbeaten Penn State when it visited Maryland. The Nits won a tough fight and in the crowded locker room afterwards, defensive tackle Doug Allen (a thoughtful young man) loomed over me, quietly stating that "not even our hometown newspaper believes in us." That team went on to an undefeated season so we couldn't have hurt the Nittany Lions too much.

The ultimate power rested with Paterno. Like most powerful coaches, Joe wanted to control the news flow. The best example came in January 1973 when New England Patriots owner Billy Sullivan offered Paterno $1.2 million to jump to the NFL. Rumors persisted for a couple of days, and on Friday of that week, New York Daily News writer Gene Ward jumped the gun and said Joe would leave, and why shouldn't he, for 10 times the money and the sake of his growing family?

I thought it over that night and agreed with Ward's logic. I called Joe's home and sports information director John Morris answered, a sure sign that something big was going on inside the Paterno household. Joe was unavailable for comment. I told John what I was going to write and he said that would be a big mistake. We were friends in many respects, and John was trying to spare me from making a fool of myself. Apparently, Joe was wavering on his decision and needed more time. My story came out in our Saturday morning paper, saying Joe was heading to New England. The university held a press conference that morning, with big news. Joe was staying! Just in time for the CDT's deadline. Joe explained that he went to bed the night before after telling his wife, Sue, that they were leaving. Neither slept well. In the morning, Joe looked at Sue and asked, "How did it feel to sleep with a millionaire?" Sue did not jump into his arms, but she may have when Joe told her they were staying. So my story was accurate until Joe and Sue awakened on Saturday morning.

I would gain some minor retribution later that winter when Penn State dropped out of the ECAC, pulling its various sports teams from their familiar conference. Paterno and his athletic department bosses wanted to break out of their Eastern bondage. I realized that this would drop the wrestling team out of its traditional rivalries with Lehigh and Navy. Wrote that story and the CDT had nothing in the afternoon. Because wrestling is a major sport in central Pennsylvania, this was a big story. Not as big as Joe staying, but it got me back on track.

This competition for stories defines what a good newspaper rivalry is about. We made each other better, and readers were more informed because of our often opposing points of view. Both sports staffs were shorthanded and worked insane hours. In my first few years at the Mirror, I started chasing stories at noon and would sometimes finish at midnight after putting the sports pages to bed. And I loved it, doing both ends of the job, back when I was young and full of enthusiasm.

One day, I interviewed Joe in the morning for a story, had two wisdom teeth extracted, and then worked until midnight, writing and editing the product. This kind of dedication is not uncommon among newspaper folks. It's called "having ink in your blood." Ron Bracken often worked similarly long hours, perhaps without his wisdom teeth coming out. The CDT staff was just Ron and veteran scribe Doug McDonald, one of the nation's most revered wrestling writers.

I guess it was the summer of 1973 when an old Collegian pal, Glenn Sheeley, called from his first newspaper job in Florida and asked if we had any openings at the Mirror. I checked with my executive editor, Paul Houck. Paul loved our sports coverage at the time and agreed to expand our staff to four people, which was a huge advantage over the CDT's two-man staff. Bracken recently told me our move gave him the leverage to get Gary Tuma switched over to sports. Gary proved to be a helluva addition to the CDT staff. But we still had them beat, 4-3, in staff size.

Glenn gave me back-up on the Penn State beat and soon surpassed my coverage. He would accept a position with the Pittsburgh Press in 1974, working the desk job at night, before suddenly landing the Steelers' beat job at the age of 25. Glenn covered Super Bowl champions in his first two seasons and moved on to Atlanta by the end of the decade. His was a natural progression up the ladder in the newspaper business while I stayed put in State

College, happy to live in a college town, write stories, and party after deadline. Glenn's departure gave me the chance to hire Dave Bloss, a Penn State student who had walked into our office one day as he neared graduation, offering his services almost for free. And Dave turned out to be another complementary piece to our staff, a smart reporter who could cover anything and get to the heart of the story. His basketball coverage set a new standard for the Mirror. Dave found a way to tell the truth about an erratic Penn State hoop program that had eluded me during my five years on the beat. He made friends with the players and somehow stayed on the right side of the head coach, John Bach, who had once warned his players not to talk to me because I was a "negative SOB."

One thing I regretted over the years is how John Andrews began to plug the increasing gaps in our work schedule by turning more to his layout skills, working until midnight almost every night to get the paper out on time, while Dennis, Bloss and I headed downtown after the phones stopped ringing. John could see that I was losing my grip. The staff still worked hard when big games came around. But we had a little more flexibility to wander.

We had friends (like the late Tucker Arnold) who would show up at our office when life got boring downtown, armed with six-packs of beer that they would place on a window sill for us to sip from while writing. The empty cans often were tossed on to the flat roof of the Mirror building after the shift ended. Later in the paper's existence, a janitor had to go up on the roof for some task and came down shaking his head. There must have been two hundred dead beer cans on the roof! Oops.

My rental home on Old Boalsburg Road became a party house, not unlike John Belushi's "Animal House" movie. When Penn State opened the 1976 football season at home against Stanford, I sent a note over to the Stanford band director, inviting his talented musicians to a party at our house. Now this was a crazy idea. The Stanford band had earned national headlines with satirical halftime shows that spoofed world figures like Mao Tse Tung. I never thought they would come. Around 7 that evening, we heard a pounding of drums off in the distance, coming closer and closer until we could see the musicians lay down their instruments on the front lawn and reach for a beer, or light up a joint.

The next morning, with beer and wine bottles tied to limbs of trees, we awakened to our next-door neighbor ringing our doorbell, waving a petition signed by half of the neighborhood, asking us to move out. We stayed for another year.

Here we have two colorful local figures, or characters, whichever you prefer, who are doing their bit at the IFC Dance Marathon to benefit the Four Diamonds Cancer Fund. The cause is worthy, you may draw your own conclusions about the contestants. At any rate, two of the entries who managed to last at least the hour that it took our photographer to get there are Kathy O'Toole, pronounced O'Toole, of the Daily Collegian, and Terry Nau, pronounced Nay-you or Now, even, he doesn't care, of the other morning newspaper locally, the Pennsylvania Mirror, pronounced Mirrow. Among the descriptions of Nau which filtered back to us were such phrases as "glassy-eyed" and "catatonic-induced appearance." Probably looked worse after he started to dance, too.

HAVING FUN – Collegian reporter Katie O'Toole and Terry Nau check out their shirts prior to start of the 1977 Dance Marathon. (Dave Hamilton photo)

You can see where this tale is headed. After four years of taking pride in my work, I let the social rumble gain ground. Summertime golf matches ended with several beers and then a late arrival to work. Wrestling tournaments with their split sessions provided respites to eat and drink. The camaraderie of friends is what brought us together but more often the beers won out. I was losing sight of my goals and closing in on the age of 30, too.

Meanwhile, rumors of the Mirror folding for financial reasons began to grow stronger. As 1977 began, I agreed to participate in the Penn State's fourth annual Dance Marathon with a Collegian reporter named Katie O'Toole whom I had met at The Phyrst, one of my favorite drinking holes. The Mirror provided good coverage for an event that was only beginning to gain a foothold in the community. Forty years later, the "THON" would annually raise millions for charity in a single weekend. In my first and only appearance, I lasted 36 hours before dropping out from exhaustion. My dance partner had finished all 48 hours in previous years but graciously walked off the floor, smiling and holding me up. Kate and I became friends for life.

My 30th birthday in late June involved a fun day of golf and many beers afterwards. Turning 30 in a college town can be depressing, especially if your future looks cloudy. I kept on going to work, sometimes stopping at bars along the way, checking my self-esteem at the door. Our new city editor, a fellow named Dave Cuzzolina, had been transferred from the parent Altoona Mirror to rein us in after Paul Houck had been fired. That was a tough assignment for Dave. We viewed him as an outsider and did not treat him well.

In early September, an edict came down from Altoona saying the Pennsylvania Mirror would cut back to two editions each week, Wednesday and Sunday, with a deadline of 10 p.m. the previous night. We would still be paid our regular salary. I was more pissed about the 10 p.m. deadline than the cutback to two days. How could we get major league baseball results into the paper?

Instinctively, I wrote a column for the first paper of the new era, headlined "Looking for the Scores?" I told the readers about our new deadline and suggested if they wanted to find out who won the baseball games last night, they should turn on the local cable TV channel and catch the scores there. The Mirror sports section was turning into a feature sheet. Time for me to leave.

I went golfing the next day and avoided work. On the following day, I walked into the office, knowing darn well my time was up. Sure enough, Cuzzolina let me know I had been fired. And that is how my 5½ years at the Mirror ended. I felt like I had quit on a principle. As the years passed, though, and I fought with another managing editor in a subsequent job, I realized that you don't win when the other guy has more power. By 1982, when I settled into a job in Pawtucket, R.I., that was handed to me by my old friends, Dave Fay and Dave Bloss, I vowed to hold my tongue, just do my job and not fight with bosses. And I lasted 30 years before getting released at age 64 in a cost-cutting layoff.

I spent a good decade missing my days at the Mirror, while maintaining old friendships with frequent trips to State College. In the mid-1980s, I finally settled down in Rhode Island with a good woman, bought a house and a dog, and continued to work those crazy newspaper hours. Cheryl and I took driving vacations around the country. Eventually we got to see Europe. I had fallen into a normal lifestyle.

Bloss and I visited Dave Fay in 2007, about a month before he succumbed to cancer, not long after he learned he had been voted into the Writers' wing of the Hockey Hall of Fame. In a reflective mood, Dave told me to enjoy my second chance at life (I just had a stent put into my heart). He was 67 when he died, happy to have made good on his own second chance.

Over the past four decades, my occasional trips from Rhode Island to Penn State for a football game required a seven-hour drive across I-95 and I-80 into Central Pennsylvania. Sometimes Dave Bloss would come along, and occasionally we would hook up with Dennis Gildea, who had become a Journalism professor at Springfield College in the Berkshire Mountains. He and "CW" found a home that backed right up to the woods. They could spot deer and an occasional black bear in the woods. T. Wes would have enjoyed the place where Dennis finished out his life.

When traveling solo, I would often get a warm feeling as the Nittany Mountains came into view. Mount Nittany is barely more than 2,000 feet high but it's big enough to seal off the region from the outside world. I took those mountains for granted when I lived inside of them. And I missed them after I left for flatter terrain.

Near the end of my long drive, John Andrews would often meet me at a restaurant in Pleasant Gap, across the street from the long-gone Big Jim's Café, one of the legendary Mirror drinking holes where the owner would leave at 2 a.m. and tell the stragglers to lock up when they left. But that was decades ago. In our later years, John and I would meet, shake hands, sit down, and order the first of several beers. The conversation would pick up where we left off, as though 1977 were just yesterday. We loved telling those old Mirror stories, chortling over our Sunday sports section and audacious coverage of minor sports like gymnastics and women's lacrosse. Sometimes we sat there for hours, reliving the past. I apologized for leaving John hanging at the office on a few occasions. He would shrug it off, take a drag from his cigarette, and tell me there's nothing to apologize for, not to him.

John had always mailed me news clippings of interest, usually sports-related, often from the Centre Daily Times, where Ron Bracken's writing and reporting became the standard of excellence for the Penn State football beat until he retired in 2008. Those news clippings stopped coming in the mail over the winter of 2016. In 2017, I received word from a mutual friend (Tom Berner) that John Andrews had died, at age 77. I didn't have the heart to attend his memorial service, preferring to remember John the way we had last left each other, a smile on each of our faces.

We were young once, and sportswriters. It was a glorious time.

CHAPTER 6
FROM PHOTOJOURNALIST TO PUBLISHER

By Terry Nau

Don Black certainly saw most of America during a newspaper career that began at the Pennsylvania Mirror as a photographer and ended in Wyoming as publisher of the Laramie Boomerang. In between the Mirror and the Boomerang, Black worked in Binghamton, N.Y., where he took a photograph of Vice President Nelson Rockefeller flipping the bird to college students that earned him a Pulitzer Prize nomination.

Employed for 19 years in the Gannett news organization, Black moved around the country, taking jobs in California, Oregon and Indiana. He split from Gannett in 1991 and went to work in Idaho before finally settling down for good in Wyoming, evolving in his career from photographer to news editor and then into management.

Like a lot of young men who came of age in the mid-1960s, Black's life was affected by the Vietnam War.

"I grew up in the suburbs of Pittsburgh," Black said over the phone from Laramie back in the spring of 2020. "Graduated from high school in 1963 and went to Penn State where I planned to major in fisheries and biology. I always liked the outdoors. But like many students in that major, classes in organic chemistry and calculus influenced me to change majors. I switched over to journalism but with the Vietnam War going on, I lost interest in school and joined the Navy."

The Navy decided Don Black should become a photographer.

"I went in for four years," Black said. "After training school, I ended up becoming the lone photographer for an Admiral's staff in Pensacola, Florida. I took pictures for all sorts of Navy publications. Whatever the staff needed, I provided. You know, I had hoped to become an outdoors writer and figured I would have to take pictures to go with my stories. The Navy pretty much immersed me in photography."

Black returned to Penn State on the G.I. Bill in August 1970. Before beginning classes, the Navy veteran applied for a job at the Pennsylvania Mirror.

"I wanted to work on the side," he recalled. "I went out to see Paul Houck at the Mirror, having no idea if there was a job available. As luck would have it, the Mirror's main photographer, Vince Calarco, had just given his notice. I walked into a wonderful job."

Black fit right into a newsroom full of young people who had more enthusiasm than experience, just like himself.

"I was a bit older (than most of the newsroom reporters)," he said. "I had experience in working on deadline from my Navy days but I did not know if my photography was good enough for a daily newspaper. I hit the ground running, taking pictures, and seeing them go into the newspaper. But I had no idea whether my work was any good or not. Finally, I pulled Tom Berner aside. He was one of the editors. We chatted a bit and then I asked Tom if I was going to make it. Tom told me, 'Are you kidding? You are knocking the lights out!' That really helped give me confidence in my abilities."

Black was the only full-time photographer on the Mirror staff and he often found himself competing against a veteran Centre Daily Times photographer, Dick Brown.

"I still had an insecurity about my work," Black admitted. "Dick Brown had already won a lot of awards for his photography. I walked into a situation where I was often competing against Dick, who was very well known even then, and probably could have worked at any newspaper in the country, he was that good. In our office, we were

HOME IN WYOMING – Pittsburgh area native Don Black always loved the outdoors. His final newspaper job took him to Wyoming, where he can fish all day. (Pete Hegg photo)

trying to beat the 'Centre Deadly' every day. If I shot a sports assignment, we would sit around the next day and compare my photos to what was in the CDT. Same for news assignments. That was a daily challenge not only for me but the entire Mirror staff. We knew the CDT dominated the market. So we would try to focus on the best story each day and make a real impact. Paul Houck talked about 'going big' but I saw it more like, to use a sports analogy, swinging for the fences. It seemed like the whole staff had confidence in each other. There was never any finger pointing.

"I learned the value of teamwork at the Mirror. If a reporter was working on a good story, he (or she) would tell me about it and we would talk about photo possibilities for that story. I learned in my future jobs that this was not always how things were done. Larger newspapers hold a lot of meetings to discuss the plan for the next day's newspaper. The Mirror's staff wasn't big enough to waste an hour with everyone sitting around in a meeting. Instead, we kicked ideas around in the newsroom. We did this without a lot of 'top-down' management. I learned that the best ideas for stories bubbled up from the bottom, rather than coming down from the top, and I used that when I went into management."

In his heart, Don Black loves the outdoors, and Central Pennsylvania more than met his desires.

"That is such a beautiful area," he said. "The best photos for me often came out in the small towns, in the rural areas, shooting pictures of farm life and agriculture. If it was deer season, I would walk into the woods and find my own shot, rather than just taking a picture of a hunter with his dead deer. I always found the natural beauty, the allure, of Central Pennsylvania to be inspiring. I would just wander around those small towns, enjoying the sights. My favorite event might have been the Grange Fair in Centre Hall, which is a small town at the bottom of the mountain.

"We covered more than Centre County. I remember when the town of Tyrone, not far from Altoona, had a big hotel fire in the middle of the winter. I think there were 12 people killed. The firemen went in to put out the fire and because the temperatures were below zero, all that water froze into ice. It took days to break up the ice and get into the hotel.

"Another time, there was a snowstorm in late September that stranded some people in the woods near a little town called Coburn. The county mobilized to get vehicles up into that town to rescue the folks who were trapped. I spent around 16 hours on the job that day."

Black never minded working long hours, even as he maintained a full course load at Penn State.

"The work was often exciting," he said. "The last thing I worried about was the hours."

Black had his own part-time assistant at the Mirror, a Penn State student named Greg Guise, who was also working his way through college, a few years behind Black.

"I was able to think about leaving the Mirror because Greg was ready to take over," Black remembered. "Greg gave me the freedom to leave without feeling like I was abandoning the team at the Mirror."

When he graduated from Penn State in June 1972, Black already had his next job lined up in Binghamton, N.Y.

"I graduated on a Saturday and went to work on Monday in Binghamton," he recalled. "I spent five and one-half years there. The biggest thing that happened to me came during the 1976 Presidential campaign when Vice President (Nelson) Rockefeller visited town with Bob Dole, who was the new Vice Presidential candidate. The local media was set up at the airport, waiting for the plane to arrive. We had our position but when the Secret Service came off the plane, they shagged all of us away from the stage area. The national media came off the press plane and tried to take over. That pissed me off. I went to the back of the hangar, looking for an oil drum to stand on, anything that would give me position above the crowd. I found a rickety old stepladder propped against the back of the hangar. I grabbed it and walked into the crowd as far as I could and got on top of the ladder. I could see the students giving

Rockefeller the business. As governor, Rockefeller had made some cuts in the state college system, and the students were still holding a grudge. They were giving him the finger and Rockefeller gave them the finger right back. That's the shot I got."

There were two Gannett papers in Binghamton at the time. The Sun-Bulletin came out in the morning and the Press in the afternoon.

"The Sun-Bulletin had first chance at my photo and ran it on page two," Black related. "The Press then used it on the front page of the second section, on what they called the local front page. There was a lot of talk about my photo. It was national news. The New York Daily News played it very big. The New York Times did not use it at all. The Buffalo paper cropped out the middle finger. By Saturday, our combined newspaper ran a story about the photo and the reaction to it. The New York Times eventually explained why they didn't use it. They said the photo did not tell the whole story because you couldn't see the kids giving Rockefeller the finger. I thought that was a Mickey Mouse explanation. The real news was Rockefeller acting the way he did."

***

Tom Berner, who went on to become a journalism professor at Penn State, wrote about his friend's photograph in a subsequent book called "Editing," published first in 1982 and revised in 1991 with the title, "The Process of Editing."

> Words cannot substitute for the good photograph. For example, in 1976 The New York Times used these words in a story about Vice President Nelson Rockefeller: "After protesters showed they were able to drown out his speech, Mr. Rockefeller then gestured three times with his finger." Did he point? Beckon? Raise his pinky? Flash the V for victory? The words don't tell. A photograph of Rockefeller gesturing was taken by Don Black, then of the Bing-

hamton, N.Y., Sun, and the photograph moved on the Associated Press and United Press International wire-photo nets. One of the papers receiving it was the Times. Rockefeller was also a former governor of New York and since he had gestured in New York, a student of journalism might assume that the Times, prideful of itself as a paper of record, would publish the photograph. Not so. The Times turned down the photograph because it was not tasteful and because the gesture could be explained in words. But the words ("... Rockefeller then gestured three times with his finger") don't make clear which finger Rockefeller gestured with or that Rockefeller gave political credibility to an obscene gesture. Even a later allusion in the story doesn't make the point the way the photograph does. The photograph makes the action credible. The reader sees it happening.

But Black doesn't hold up the Rockefeller photograph as his finest. In fact, he says he was in the right place at the right time and was not even sure Rockefeller had made the gesture or if it was on film. When Black, now managing editor of the Lafayette, Indiana, Journal and Courier, discusses his work, he cites another of his photos about a father delivering his wife's baby as an example of a good photograph, one he is pleased with. Black likes that photograph because "it is more universal — it's a look at a facet of life that needs no words to augment it, and the communication and impact don't depend on who these people are, but on what is happening. If the mayor of Binghamton rather than the vice president had given `the finger' to the crowd that day, there would have been no interest outside of our circulation area. The birth picture, on the other hand, has been published all over the world in numerous magazines and is a better example of the type of involvement and communication I would like to see in all my pictures."

***

By 1978, Black had moved on to the San Bernardino Sun newspaper in California.

"They made me director of photography," Black said. "The Sun was one of the leaders in photo journalism at the time. But after two years, I had a chance to go work in Salem, Oregon, not far from where my wife Terrie's parents lived. It was great for me, too, because of the outdoors and the fishing available up there. During my time in Salem, I went from photo editor to photo director and then to features editor, news editor on the copy desk and finally to night managing editor."

Black's time with Gannett was coming to an end. The chain next assigned him to Lafayette, Indiana, as managing editor but he soon had the itch to go back West.

"I left Lafayette, and Gannett, after two years and took a managing editor's job in Pocatello, Idaho. That ended 19 years at Gannett for me. I stayed in Pocatello until 1998 when I moved 25 miles north for my first publisher's job at the Blackfoot Morning News.

Within three years, Black would be recruited by the Laramie Boomerang, where he finished his 42-year newspaper career in 2012.

Don's wife, Terrie, died in 2019.

"Terrie was with me the whole way," Black said. "We were married in 1967 when I was still in the Navy."

Looking back on his life, Black admitted that his love for the outdoors has been a constant presence.

"At the Mirror, sometimes I would take off for lunch while my film was drying, and go fishing at a place called Fisherman's Paradise, which was not far down the road. It was a great way to relax in the middle of my work day. I always loved the outdoors. Even as a kid, I enjoyed hunting and fishing. I hiked a lot. But I never really experienced great fishing until I came to Central Pennsylvania."

Ironically, Don Black stopped taking photographs as he switched over to newspaper management.

"I became so tied up in editing, fighting for resources and participating in community events that I failed to keep up with the changing technology in photography. Everything is digital now."

With the passing of years, Black can reflect from his fishing hole on a career that took him all over the country, from Pennsylvania and central New York to California, Oregon, and Indiana, before returning to the west and his final job in Wyoming. Don Black is living out his years in a place he loves.

"I can still stop in at the Boomerang whenever I want and help the paper by writing local editorials as needed," he said.

And among his memories, Black cites his first newspaper job as an important step in his career.

"I look back on the Pennsylvania Mirror as a special place," Black recalled. "I loved working there, making some great friends and living in Central Pennsylvania, such a beautiful place."

CHAPTER 7
FROM BEDFORD TO BERLIN

By Terry Nau

Greg Guise grew up in the small southwestern Pennsylvania town of Bedford (population, less than 3,100). As fate would have it, he fell under the spell of a local newspaper editor who would shape his career as a photographer and film editor. Greg's career would first take him to the Pennsylvania Mirror and then on to Altoona where he switched over to television. Greg wound up working for CBS and WUSA TV in the nation's capital.

TRAVELING MAN – *Greg Guise went from newspaper to television work during his long career in journalism. (Photo courtesy of Greg Guise)*

When asked to speak about his career, Greg goes back to the lessons he learned in Bedford and with the ambitious Mirror newspaper in State College, Pa.

"When I was a junior in high school," Guise recalled in the spring of 2020, "I was friends with the family of the Bedford Gazette's city editor, a man named Terry Leach, who was a 1957 journalism graduate of Penn State. Terry was my mentor. He did more for my career than anyone. I watched him do everything at his paper. He reported on town meetings, wrote stories, took photos, laid out the pages. He was a real jack of all trades. I watched him work and thought, 'This is what I want to do.'"

Working for Terry Leach, Greg picked up basic skills in newspaper photography. He studied hard in school and was accepted to the main campus at Penn State in 1970.

"I didn't have much money," he remembered. "I knew I would have to work part-time while going to college. Terry Leach knew of the new Pennsylvania Mirror paper and suggested I stop by the office to drop off a resume. Luckily, they had a part-time opening for a photographer. Don Black was the head photographer and he hired me to work 20 hours per week. The Mirror had an offset printing press, and that was pretty new at the time. It was one of the few newspapers in the country running color photographs. And the newspaper covered a big part of Central Pennsylvania. Its circulation area included Centre, Blair, Huntingdon and Mifflin counties. I could drive almost anywhere to take photographs.

"The Mirror did a good job of covering spot news. We would hear about a train derailment or bad car crash and go after the photo. We covered Hurricane Agnes in the summer of 1972 when there was flooding everywhere. A roommate of mine at the time was visiting Denver. He saw one of my photos of the flood coverage on the front page of the Rocky Mountain News (via the Associated Press). When the flooding finally ended, the Mirror put out a special section of 42 pages on Hurricane Agnes that won some awards."

Shooting color was a complicated process in those days.

"This was before digital cameras or even auto focus lenses," Guise said. "For color assignments, we often shot staged events so that everything would be easier to get into focus. There were two ways at the time to shoot color – slides or negatives. We used the

SPECIAL SECTION –
The Pennsylvania Mirror combined its daily coverage of Hurricane Agnes into a 42-page section back in 1972. (Greg Guise photo)

system of shooting slides, or transparencies, as they were called. Then we would go out to a color lab in Bellefonte to get them developed. I believe the fellow who ran the lab was named Les Shaw. We would 'soup' the film at Les's lab. The development process with color had to be next to perfect. It's very easy to overexpose or underexpose your film and you are left with something that doesn't look too good. This was a good learning experience for me."

Guise also shot Penn State football games in color, honing his skills for action photography.

"I remember taking a photo of Joe Paterno with Rip Engle for one of the early Sunday editions (in 1972)," Guise recalled. "Rip had been the head coach at Penn State before Joe and they were great friends. I wish I still had the originals of that photo because I would love to hang the picture in my house." (Forty seven years later while in search for material for this book, Guise uncovered a print of the picture and is in the process of digitally remastering it.)

When Don Black took a job in Binghamton in 1972, Guise moved into the full-time position, head photographer.

"This job was big time for me," Guise said. "I could do some free-lancing and make extra money on the side. Of course, we had a lot of work to do at the Mirror. We tried to publish color photos at least three times a week, including every Thursday. That's when the auto ads all ran, some of them in color, and we would have color on page one that the auto ads basically subsidized.

"The Mirror was a small newspaper with big ambitions," Guise added. "I guess there was more talent there because it was a college town. The CDT had a great photographer in Dick Brown, who was more of an artistic photographer than a hard news guy. The big advantage we had at the Mirror was the quality of our offset printing press. The CDT had an older press and their reproduction was not always good. Our photos usually looked pretty sharp."

Guise was able to stretch his wings under Mirror editor Paul Houck.

"Paul was a bit misunderstood in those days but when I looked back after I worked other places, I began to understand him better,"

Guise said. "Paul always defended the newsroom. He did a good job of enforcing what I call the *Chinese wall* between the newsroom and advertising. He fought for the independence of the newsroom, and that was absolutely critical. I remember he had a shovel attached to a frame in his office. The plaque said, 'This is a spade. Call it that.' We used to laugh about that shovel but it was what Paul believed. Tell the truth.

"One thing Paul taught me to do was to 'go big.' He wasn't afraid to make big decisions, like starting the Sunday sports tabloid, or doing a big section on Hurricane Agnes. That philosophy of going big was something I always remembered and used through the rest of my career."

That philosophy came to fruition in 1974 during an oil embargo that seriously impacted the nationwide trucking business.

"As an AP stringer, I had developed a good working relationship with AP photographer Paul Vathis, who became another mentor to me," Guise admitted. "When truckers staged shut-downs to protest high diesel prices, hundreds of rigs blocked Interstate 80 near the Lamar exit, about 25 miles from State College. Vathis and I set up a remote darkroom in a bathroom at the local truck stop. We wired photos to the Mirror and to media outlets across the country."

Guise left the Mirror in 1976 for a job in television with Channel 10 in Altoona, about 40 miles down Route 220 from State College.

"A couple of my friends from the local radio stations – Jon McClintock and Eric Rabe – took jobs with Channel 10," Guise said. "They said to me: Why don't you give television a try? I found I really enjoyed shooting film. It was an interesting job, to shoot an assignment and then come back and edit the film down to what they needed to use on the air."

While shooting an assignment in nearby Johnstown, Guise fell into the chance of a lifetime.

"There was a hockey movie called Slap Shot with Paul Newman under production at the War Memorial ice rink in Johnstown," Guise said. "The producers told me they needed a couple of photographers for a scene in the movie where Newman throws them out of the locker room. It all came together pretty quickly. I drove down the next day, they put some makeup on me, and then the director tells me I have to push Paul Newman a little bit. He said, 'You have to get into a shoving match because they are throwing you out of the locker room.' We finished the scene in two takes. It's funny. I have done a lot of things in my career but everyone always asks me about that movie, which is still popular to this day. It is kind of a cult film for people who love hockey."

The experience stays with Guise, if only because he could add Paul Newman to the list of celebrities he met during his career.

"The movie people were nice to us," he said. "Newman, too. I did not know what to expect going in. I had covered celebrities before, for example when Jimmy Carter ran for President, he came to central Pennsylvania a couple of times. Paul Newman, though, he's pretty high on the list for me."

Guise left Altoona for another television job in Detroit, stayed a couple of years, and then moved on to the nation's capital, where he worked for the local CBS station, CBS bureau and sometimes with the national news show. He finished his career working for Al Jazeera's English channel, covering all of North America.

"It sounds much bigger than it really is," he said. "I have probably been in the Oval Office a hundred times for photo ops. They whisk you in and out pretty quickly. George Bush is probably the only President who knew my name. So much of what happens in official Washington is choreographed. I much preferred working on news stories for the local affiliate, WTOP (later WUSA9) where I could shoot and edit my material. We staffed the national political conventions every four years. I was assigned to cover Hurricane Hugo. And I was sent to Germany to cover the fall of the Berlin Wall in 1989. But it wasn't as exciting as it sounds. I was stuck two blocks away from the Brandenburg Gate, sitting in a video truck, editing tape. I didn't see much of the wall coming down."

Greg Guise and his wife returned to State College after he retired from the news business. He still keeps in touch with old friends, and sometimes he thinks back to his days as a kid in Bedford, working at the local newspaper, learning the craft. He still considers the late Terry Leach as his mentor, and stays in touch with his widow. That initial newspaper experience in his hometown, and his five years with the Mirror, were the foundation for Greg's career.

"I look at my time with the Mirror as cultivation," he said. "It was like a fertilizer where I worked on improving and growing my skills. I was a young kid trying to learn from the people in that newsroom."

CHAPTER 8
HOOKED ON A BYLINE

By Robert Emmers

Oct. 19, 1971 was a beautiful fall day, crisp air, blue skies, warm sun. (If I remember correctly, that is, impending tragedy somehow requiring, in my memory's effort at foreshadowing, the opposite of cinematic gloom.) I had just returned to my office on High Street in Bellefonte – this was the local bureau of the Centre Daily Times – from a brief walk. I was back at my desk pecking away on my ancient upright typewriter and trying to breathe despite the fog of cigarette smoke another reporter was spewing forth like the fumes from a coal plant. (Oh, that typewriter: an ancient Underwood, I think, already probably thirty years old, and I wish I'd somehow managed to take it with me when I moved from that office because if it was an antique then it would be even more of an antique now, worth $900 or more, although I never would have sold it; it would be sitting on a corner of my desk, staring across at my computer screen and al-

HOOKED ON WRITING –
From his days as a Boy Scout, Robert Emmers wanted to write.

ways reminding me, not of that particular day, but of all the days back then when being reporter was so much fun I might have done it for free – and given the size of my paycheck I practically did.)

Anyway, there were several loud popping sounds from out on the street, sounds that were, for me then, mysterious and thus requiring investigation. From the office I ran up High Street to the commotion of a crowd at the intersection with Allegheny Street near the Courthouse. What I gathered from the excited bystanders, who were watching the efforts of several people tending to two fallen figures across the street, was that a man had driven up High Street, stopped just short of Allegheny Street, opened fire with a rifle on two policeman directing traffic and then sped away up the hill past the Courthouse and the jail. Back in the office, nearly out of breath, I called the Times city room in the main office in State College (it was on Fraser Street back then, across from the borough building), then headed back outside where I ran into a freelance photographer we often employed. We jumped into his car, which was equipped with a police scanner, and speeded up the High Street hill following the shooter's path. From the scanner we learned that the police were following the shooter out of town, so near the top of the hill we turned right, thinking to get down to East Bishop Street and follow the pursuit.

As we turned, we were broadsided by a township police car running through a stop sign without lights or siren.

I ended up in the emergency room, waiting while the trauma team worked to save the police officers whose shooting had sparked the whole business. (The wounds to Bellefonte Officer Ronald Seymore proved fatal. The other officer, Clarence Seward, survived.) Meanwhile, The Times editor, Jerry Weinstein, assigned veterans, old timers, to Big Foot me, to take over the story, what I thought of as *my* story. And thus, at the age of 22, despite the extreme pain in my ribs and arm, and despite the sadness at the deaths, this newspaper neophyte lost *his* Big Story, his first Big Story, and felt his self-esteem plummet and in the process learned *his* first Big Lesson of the newspaper trade: Every story you work on becomes immensely personal and because of that every newspaper you ever work for will break your heart at one time or the other.

***

I'm going to tell you what it was like beginning a newspaper career in small town America 50 years ago, a time when newspapers, to say nothing of truth and accuracy, still mattered. It was also a time for me to begin my passage across the boundary of experiences that, Conrad wrote in *Shadow-Line*, marks the journey from youth to maturity. But before I begin, I want to offer a bit of advice to any young person who might be reading this while mulling his or her career choices. If, among the careers you're contemplating, is that of journalism, just forget it! The golden age of newspapering through which I and my contemporaries passed is long gone and will not be repeated. But if you ignore this advice and manage to graduate with a degree in (God forbid) journalism or communications and if you are then lucky enough to get a job on a newspaper, you'll be paid a pittance and anyone who might have imparted reporting or editing wisdom to you will be long gone through layoffs or buy-outs. But, you say, I spent all that money and all those years earning a degree and I really want to be a reporter. Oh, you poor sod, you have been captured by the myth! There are only a handful of enterprises that still count, newspapers or websites or broadcast outlets, the New York Times, the Wall Street Journal, the Washington Post, the networks and your chances of landing there as a neophyte are infinitesimally small.

As an alternative, you could go into public relations and spend the rest of your career writing nifty jingles for soap or vitamin supplements or cereal filled with salt and sugar while supporting the bottom line of a multinational company which doesn't care a fig about people. Or, if you are reasonably good-looking with all of your teeth and most of your hair, you could maybe get a job on a local TV station where you'll dream of making it big and going on to the networks but twenty years later you'll still be running your butt off covering ten stories a day, all of them involving traffic accidents, meth lab explosions or the latest fad involving what the young people are ingesting or smoking or shooting themselves up with at the moment.

So just don't. Give it up. Get a degree in something interesting like literature so that in your old age when you're trying to scrape by on whatever's left of Social Security you'll at least be able to make an informed pick at the library, assuming there are any libraries left, or from Amazon if you decide you'd rather read a book than have a decent meal. Or better yet, get a degree in computer science so you can at least get a coding job — as a contractor without benefits, of course — between recessions.

Anyway, as for me, I fell into newspapering basically by accident. I was a Boy Scout and needed a couple more merit badges to reach Eagle rank. Since I wanted to write, the journalism merit badge seemed a safe choice that wouldn't require a great deal of work: anyway, a lot less work than swimming a mile or building a bridge out of rope and tree branches. Now, the counselor for journalism merit badge was Jerry Weinstein, the editor of our local newspaper, the Centre Daily Times. In those days fifty or more years ago, the editor of the local newspaper was a leader of the community, a shaper of public opinion, someone who did business at the pinnacle, and so I was more than a little apprehensive about meeting Mr. Weinstein. (But as it turned out, he was probably just as nervous as I was: while he'd been the journalism merit badge counselor for years, I learned later, I was the first Scout to seek him out, his first victim, in other words, and he must have wondered just what he was supposed to do with this wide-eyed young neophyte looking to him for wisdom.)

When I finally made it to his office, I expected to face some gruff, no-nonsense type, a take-no-prisoners sort as befitted my conception of a newspaper editor, gleaned chiefly from old movies like *Deadline USA* and *-30-*. My first impression seemed to match that expectation: here before me was a tall, broad-shouldered, scowling 40-ish character with thick black hair and, of course, the requisite cigarette in hand. (Everybody smoked in those days.) But when he shook my hand and smiled, I suddenly realized that he bore a striking resemblance to the writer J. D. Salinger, whose novel *Catcher in the Rye* I'd re-read several times. (Teenage angst and alienation!) How could anyone who looked like J. D. Salinger, a person whom I greatly admired, be anything close to an ogre?

And, of course, he wasn't. He soon had me reporting and writing stories, which he would go through, telling me in an even manner what was good and what was bad. He'd put together a talented newsroom – John Brutzman, Paul Dubbs (who knew every nook and cranny of the county), John Kurilla, that excellent writer and editor Bill Welch, among others – and I spent time with all of them. They were welcoming and generous with advice, but I found myself not feeling the excitement I thought I would feel, here in this domain of real adults performing real jobs. It was just that everything seemed subdued; where was the wise-cracking banter among hardened, visor-wearing editors; where was the violent cursing of reporters trying to pry information from recalcitrant officials; where were the shouts of "Copy boy!" or the frenzied clamor of bells announcing the arrival of some wire service bulletin. (It took me awhile to understand that only scattered moments in any newsroom are filled with *Sturm und Drang*. And to be honest, I initially overlooked the fact that Welch did in fact wear a visor as he hewed away at copy with his thick orange pencil.)

Strangely, it was when Jerry took me on a tour of the composing room, filled with its heady aroma of hot lead, ink and cigarette smoke, that the bug finally bit me. These were the days before the wide-spread use of computers, so the composing room was filled with the clatter of the linotypes – those huge machines that created the lines of type – and the clacking of lead as the compositors filled up their galley trays with the fodder the linotypes spit out. Jerry and I were standing behind one of the linotypes, watching its operator bang away at the keyboard with incredible speed as the machine whirred and groaned assembling the molds which would then mechanically set a single line of type, a slug, from the molten metal.

Shortly thereafter, Jerry presented me with a special slug: my byline cast in a shiny piece of lead.

I was totally hooked.

***

My first actual paying job at the Centre Daily Times (hereinafter the CDT) involved compiling the bowling scores and then writing a paragraph that would appear atop the scores. Exciting and challenging, huh? No, not really, but the sports editor, Doug McDonald, was always kind and forbearing with any mistakes, and so, it was a start, tentative and groping, but a start. I kept that lead slug bearing my byline in my pocket and later on my desk, when I got a desk, and eventually I graduated into a real reporting job. On a small newspaper like the CDT most of the reporting consists of going to the meetings of government authorities, the borough council, the planning commission, the county commission and the like, interspersed with coverage of the occasional fire or car wreck or flood or hunting accident, all the while waiting for a chance at The Big Story. My chance arrived, I thought, with the Tressler shooting in Bellefonte, but I was quickly removed courtesy of a township police car and would have been Big Footed out of it in any case. (There's an amusing denouement to this tale. Sometime after the uproar had died, I was back in my High Street office when I was visited by an adjuster for the insurance company that provided coverage to the township. He handed me a release and a check for, if memory serves – and who knows if it really does – $900, not a fortune but also nothing to sneeze at in those days. Knowing what I know now, having journeyed out into the wide world, I should have enlisted a lawyer and held out for something more princely. But what did I know? I was a kid. So sure, I said, and signed the release and accepted the check. Which I immediately turned over to Jerry Weinstein. After all, the paper had covered my medical expenses.)

But if I missed the coverage of the shooting itself, there was still John Tressler's trial for murder. This took place in the Centre County Courthouse, that imposing edifice with its Greek Revival façade, a few blocks from my office. This was my first murder trial, and the long, wide, high-ceilinged court room with its formidable judge's bench made me feel even younger than I was. (Of course, one of the purposes of a courtroom is to make those attending feel insignificant in the face of the law, especially a defendant; the architecture, however, seemed to have no effect on John Tressler, who scowled defiantly from behind the defense table.) Sitting there with my pen and notepad (no computers or cell phones in those days), I was looking forward to all the shenanigans and maneuvers I had come to expect from watching court dramas on TV, but in the end the trial proved to consist of long stretches of more or less boring testimony regarding what everybody already knew because they had seen it first hand, interspersed with occasional clashes among District Attorney Chuck Brown, defense attorney Bill Clinard and Judge R. Paul Campbell.

Now, the CDT was an afternoon paper back then, meaning early deadlines, so I would sit nervously through the morning court session, hoping for something that would give me a story, then hurtle down High Street to the office to file. But there was no time to type out a story, think about it, make changes. Breathlessly, I had to plop myself in front of the keyboard of the teletype that connected our office with the main office in State College and immediately start banging away. It was pretty much an exercise in automatic writing and I'm not sure I really knew what I'd written until I could see the edited version in that evening's paper. Thank God for a good editor like Bill Welch.

***

Afternoon newspapers were slowly dying away, in large part, I've always thought, because the TV networks were expanding their evening news programs. The CDT itself would convert to morning publication in the late 80s. But Centre County had a morning newspaper long before that. Yes, children, I'm finally getting around to the Pennsylvania Mirror, memoriam of which is a major point of this exercise, no?

The Pennsylvania Mirror sprang from the nearly 100-year-old womb of the Altoona Mirror in late 1968. The idea was that it would plop onto your doorstep in the early hours so you could pick it up and read all the sports scores from the night before while you drank your breakfast coffee instead of having to wait until the cocktail hour when the scores in the afternoon paper were almost a day late. Of course, it was also about more than just the sports scores. The Mirror would employ the latest composing and printing technology, feature lots of color and photos, cover whatever was important in central Pennsylvania, not shy away from irreverence and, whenever possible, speak truth to power. Thus, tons of advertising would be drawn away from the stodgy CDT. This notion incorporated enough hubris to fuel a play by Sophocles, but does not mean, of course, that it was a reckless one, at least for the Big Money boys (and girls.)

Around this time, the late 60s, I was sticking my toes into the waters of a return to college but quickly shouting Yikes before pulling my toes out of said water. Or maybe more travel was in order. (I'd already hitched two-thirds of the way around the world.) I briefly worked on Robert Kennedy's presidential campaign, lucked out with a high number in the draft, joined and then was fired by VISTA (after organizing a protest at a Bureau of Indian Affairs office in Colorado), thought about becoming a professional bowler and, here and there, participated in various protests, in other words basically all the things young people were doing at the time. Eventually, I settled in as a reporter for the CDT.

And then, sometime in 1972, I left the CDT and went to work at the Mirror.

Why this happened remains something of a mystery to me, although I've never regretted the move. It might have had something to do with money: The Mirror offered me more of it. But my suspicion is that I simply felt trapped. Youth, after all, is both restless and reckless. I found myself looking at the future and what I saw was that after twenty years covering those borough council and planning commission meetings, interspersed with the occasional coverage of a massive car accident or natural disaster, I'd switch over to editing – I'd be the guy with the green eye shade and the thick orange pencil.

And then in another twenty years I'd retire.

And then I'd die.

Because that seemed like a nightmare, was it any wonder I made the switch to The Mirror? (I do have to say, however, that leaving the CDT was not without feelings of guilt; in some ways, it seemed a betrayal of Jerry Weinstein, who had been very good to me. Probably there lurked in the recesses of my brain the notion that someday I would return to my first newspaper home. But those same convoluted recesses of my brain must have realized this would probably never happen: that I was just trying to justify my own lust for the new and exciting.)

***

I don't know if you remember, but the 70s were a damn wacky decade. I mean, any decade that can manage to combine Hard Hats, Kent State, Monty Python, nitrous whippets, Jimmy Carter's lust in his heart and lava lamps has to make the list of top crazy decades. (And no, I'm not just having acid flashbacks.)

It also made it the perfect time to work at The Mirror.

What a noble – or crazy – experiment, taking on the area's long-entrenched and dominant daily. As I said before, to the bean counters in Altoona it had to have seemed an experiment worth doing, but I think that after the first couple of heady years, those of us who worked at The Mirror knew it couldn't really last. One of my signature memories of my time there is when we folks on the news side got together and ran an ad in Editor and Publisher magazine offering an entire "staff for sale." I'm sure that brought a chuckle to editors seeking employees, and in part, it *was* tongue in cheek. But it had its serious aspect as well: despite going about our business as fervently as always, we were also seeing that ghostly hand chalking its message on the wall. (In hindsight, I have some regrets at instigating the whole escapade. Publisher Blair Bice and Executive Editor Paul Houck were both fine men and good executives and didn't deserve what must have seemed like our lack of faith in them. It wasn't meant that way, but still. By the way, we did get some responses to our ad, but nothing particularly serious.)

We know, of course, how the story ended: The Mirror ceased publication in 1977, despite the best efforts of all involved. By then I had escaped, but not because I regretted my switch from the CDT. The Mirror city room was the place where I honed both my craft and my attitude. There were so few of us – five or six, not counting the sports and photograph people – that even though I had my regular beats I had to be ready to cover everything and anything, from the county commissioners to the Black-lung travails of retired miners. There was a freedom in this that conferred equal responsibility, and I found myself moving toward, if not yet across, that shadow line of Conrad's I spoke of earlier, that boundary between youth and maturity. I came to feel that what I was doing was something more than just earning a paycheck, that conveying the news required digging deep and trying to get at the essential meaning of what was going on, whether it had to do with the State College By-pass and what of our history that long concrete slab would bury, a big local issue at the time, or some planning commission's zoning action that might seem trivial on the face of it but which could have a profound effect on residential home values.

Much of this had to do with the times in which we were living: the Watergate years. Almost every night, Dave Fay, who was our editor, would rip the latest Watergate story off the clattering wire machine and, standing behind his horseshoe desk, read us the top of the latest reporting by Seymour Hersh or the boys and girls at the Washington Post and the New York Times. It was heady stuff. Of course, we at The Mirror weren't working on anything as critically important as presidential abuse of power or the Vietnam War or the legal battle over the Pentagon Papers. But we were going after local issues with a kind of zeal that had never really been apparent, at least to me, at the CDT.

I was still at the CDT when the flooding from Hurricane Agnes submerged a wide swatch of central Pennsylvania. The Mirror put together a package of coverage, both words and photos, that was particularly exceptional. Also pre-dating my time at The Mirror was the paper's great coverage of the moon landing. (This even pre-dated my CDT tenure; at the time I was working at Mid-State Airport, manning the rental car desk and, between flights, hauling the airmail to Clearfield and Phillipsburg.) The Agnes floods and the moon landing were events that don't come around every year, and so much of what we were focused on were the routine doings of local government. Ah, but what energy we brought to it, enough to warm the hearts of Woodward and Bernstein.

Sometimes, I confess, a little too much energy, generally on my part. One night I was working the phones trying to dig out information about some action taken by a township board of supervisors – Spring Township, I think, although I do not remember the particular issue. I finally managed to get one of the supervisors on the phone and started asking my questions, gradually zeroing in on the issue I'd called about. For some reason the action by the supervisors troubled me greatly, and I asked the man on the phone why the board had acted in this manner. I don't remember the man's name, but he must have been an ordinary, part-time public servant doing the best he could, and I can remember thinking that I ought to be treating him a little less confrontationally. But then, in reply to one of my questions, he said, "Wait a minute! You can't write about that!" or words to that effect. And this set me off. For a good five minutes I lectured him about open meetings and open records and the responsibilities of a free press and the public's right to know and how dare he tell me I couldn't report on this issue and so on and so forth.

(If that sounds awfully self-righteous to you, rest assured it hit me the same way – but unfortunately not until an hour or so later when we had all our copy in and I had time to think about what had happened. I didn't call the supervisor back and apologize, my excuse being that it was too late; besides, the more I thought about it, the more I came to the conclusion that the motive behind my outburst had been a good one – it was indeed time for local officials to understand they couldn't keep their doings secret; it was just that the way I'd gone about trying to obtain the information was not particularly effective. Maybe, I thought, instead of lecturing and, as my grandmother would have put it, getting up on my high horse, I might have better achieved my goal with a friendlier, calmer approach. I did eventually, as I proceeded in my career, become an excellent interviewer, but whether I owe that to the incident with the township supervisor, I don't know.)

There was another incident while I was at The Mirror that influenced my mindset as a reporter and later as an editor. (Yes, I became one of that hated species.) I was sent out to cover an ongoing police situation and arrived to find a number of state police officers surrounding a gunman holed up in a house. Every so often the man would appear at the doorway, waving a firearm and threatening to kill himself if the police didn't leave him alone. This went on for hours; it grew dark and cold. The gunman made one of his regular appearances and once more threatened to shoot himself unless the police left. Exhausted and frustrated, the state police corporal in charge of the scene shouted back, "Jesus, then just go ahead and do it!"

The gunman put the firearm to his head and killed himself.

This denouement occurred way past deadline, too late to make the morning's paper. The next day the subject of how to handle the situation became the subject of internal discussion among the editors. In the midst of this, the commander of the state police barracks called and asked that we not include in our coverage what the corporal said to the gunman, which might have spurred him to suicide. The commander's argument was this: yes, the corporal made a bad decision and would be counseled and punished for it, but he was an outstanding officer with a good future ahead of him and if we published what happened, it would destroy his career. A valid point. On the other hand, didn't the public have a right to know about something that could affect their safety if this officer were to react similarly in a future situation? The details of our internal discussions are lost to me now, but I suspect the final decision to kill the story was made by Paul Houck, the executive editor, and involved a great deal of soul searching; after all it was his job to get stories into the paper, not necessarily to keep them out. And it was a good story. To this day, I'm not sure I agree with killing it, but I do know that Paul's decision took into account the effects on all involved and was not made frivolously. What it took was mental anguish of a sort I would only learn later when I was an editor myself.

***

What sticks in my memory most notably from my time at The Mirror? For one thing, the fact that The Mirror gave me the freedom to pursue stories that interested me but weren't necessarily on my beat. Let's see. I got a tip that the historic State College Hotel was a conflagration just waiting the errant flip of a match or the squirm of a frayed electrical connection to burst into devastating fire. The Alpha Fire Company was so aware of the danger, my tipster reported, that in the event the building caught fire, their plan was to demolish adjacent buildings if necessary to halt the blaze. So, I snuck into the rambling building with a photographer and found piles of trash, fire doors blocked open, alarms that didn't work and so forth. (Be aware that this was the condition of the hotel 45 years ago, not today.) Let's see further: There was turmoil in the United Mine Workers, and I journeyed north to learn the experiences of retired miners fighting Black lung disease. I followed the race for representative from the 23rd Congressional District, which then included Centre County. (Me: Congressman, what about this donation from XYZ bank? Rep. Albert Johnson: That? That's peanuts; they couldn't buy me for that!) What else? The environmental effects of highway construction projects. Rock climbing. The travails of Westinghouse Kyles, genius, music lover, accused murderer. The intricacies of zoning law. The 1973 truckers' strike. (There I was in a front-page photo in the CDT, surrounded by truckers striding forward to meet the Governor. Ha ha ha, take that, CDT.) A letter from a friend named Steven, with whom I used to drink stout and sing sad songs, who had escaped to Dublin. (A story I find more than a little embarrassing now, but the freedom to pursue is also the freedom to totally screw up the chase.)

For another thing, that small and excellent band of city-side reporters: Jean Reeve, Denise Bowman, Perri Foster-Pegg (whose flamboyant name I could often not quite manage, sometimes calling her Foster Perri-Pegg), and Sheila Irvine, whose moving profile of John Tressler's wife is firmly lodged in my brain. And, of course, the photogs Don Black, Greg Guise and Dave Hamilton and the sports guys, Terry Nau and Dennis Gildea (and others whose names I've forgotten. My apologies for a faulty memory.)

And one more thing my memory will never let loose: the My-Oh-My.

Every newspaper has a bar – or used to anyway – and the My was ours. This was back in the day before hipsters, horrendous traffic, McMansions and pretentious sorts of all types filled up the nice little valley oasis of State College. This was back in the day when there were still good dive bars and the My was ours. The My stretched between College Avenue and Calder Alley, narrow and dark and smoky. Half of the My, the half with an entrance off College Avenue, was a gay bar. The other half, its entrance off Calder Alley, was a topless bar with a dancer in the corner, occasionally visible through the cigarette haze.

There's a photo of The Mirror staff standing in front of the Benner Pike building, proudly holding our state press association awards. There are more than twenty people in that photo. Good Lord, I thought, who are all those people? Stringers, occasional contributors and a couple CDT retirees, I suppose, because my memory is of that newsroom of half a dozen city-side reporters and editors, and down at the other end of the room the sports guys. We'd all be smoking and talking furiously, on the phone or to each other or cursing our IBM Selectrics because we'd hit the wrong key and entered an unsuitable code that would infuriate the optical character reader and screw up the type-setting equipment. Then, around 11 pm or so, a relative quiet would descend. Us city-side types would pack up and head downtown to the My. (The sports guys had their own, beer-drinking rituals which they maintained in the emptying newsroom.) If we'd close down the My, we'd then head to someone's house to play poker and listen to old Marty Robbins records.

But, the My.

Great times there, although for the most part what exactly those great times involved remain locked up in a now rarely visited beer-and-cigarette fumed corner of my brain. But there is one memory that always resounds: Jack Sapia's pronouncements.

Jack was the owner and manager of the My. What I see, when I think of him, is a robust, round-faced man, with big glasses and black, black hair. But I'm not seeing him so much as hearing him. We'd generally gather around a table against the back wall that separated us from the gay bar, although we'd sometimes sneak around the corner, because the gay bar could be less crowded and the beer cheaper. We'd come roistering in, and eventually Jack would make his way over to our table. He'd stand there, staring at us. We would wait for one of his pronouncements.

If he was particularly vexed — by the downtown traffic, by the idiot students who didn't understand the meaning of crosswalks or red lights, by some moronic decision from the borough authorities

— he'd put his hands on his hips and say, loudly: "State College, Pa, a horseshit town."

Other times, for no particular reason, he would say, disparagingly, "French-cut green beans!" The context of that remains a mystery to me.

Then Jack would wander away, and we'd furiously drink more beer and argue loudly about some event or some story or the latest political outrage. Then we'd drink more beer.

The My.

***

We're near the end, and frankly, I'm tired remembering. What's particularly exhausting is the recall of all those faces of my youth. Sheila, Denise, Perri, Jean, Dave, Greg, Paul, Terry, Dennis, and others. I haven't kept up with them, and that's my failing, but at least in that way I'm not confronted with aging faces that have to be as worn as my own.

It was my good fortune to begin my journalism career at a time when newspapers were still a vital part of their communities. I was equally fortunate to come up at a time when one's skills at reporting, writing and editing were more important than a college degree, which I did not have. My goal became to work for a major metro, and that meant working my way up the hierarchy of newspapers. I left The Mirror in 1976 and moved to a small daily in upstate New York as managing editor and editorial writer, working for a mean and crazy publisher who made me appreciate all the more the understated manner of Blair Bice, The Mirror publisher. From there I went to the Billings (MT) Gazette, where I worked on investigative projects involving land fraud and was once threatened by a gun-toting shyster. Then it was on to the Norfolk Virginian-Pilot as city editor, the Detroit Free Press as a feature writer, and eventually to the Orange County (CA) Register where I worked on investigative projects involving organized crime and later wrote a column. Major metros at last!

But after that things got a little crazy as mid-life caught up with me. For a while I worked as a private investigator and then a fraud investigator for a major insurance company. Newspapering drew me again and I edited California's premier legal newspaper. That attracted the attention of the owner of what is, arguably, the best crisis communications firm in the country. (Most of the firm's members were former reporters and editors like me. And, like me, most of them ended up there for the money. What you come to realize after a long journalism career is that this is not the optimal method for setting aside a retirement nest egg.)

And now? Retired and back in Pennsylvania. Retired, however, is an inexact concept. Golf? Bingo? Hardly. I work full-time at my computer, but the product is not journalism; rather I'm now what I dreamed of being as a teenager, a writer of fiction, publishing short stories and working on a novel. (Yes, a writer of fiction, but in DuBois, rather than Paris. The small nest egg I finally managed to acquire would not stretch as far as those teenage dreams desired.)

And so, we come to the end of the tale. Here I would very much like to fashion an ending tying everything into a neat bundle with The Mirror at its many-wrapped core. But life isn't that tidy. If it hadn't been for Boy Scouts and the need for one more merit badge, I might not have met Jerry Weinstein and eventually been handed that life-changing slug of lead bearing my by-line. If I hadn't been miffed about something or the other, I might have stayed at the Centre Daily Times and retired forty-five years later (as the editor?) instead of hauling myself down the Benner Pike to The Mirror building. And if the money boys had come up with enough dough to keep The Mirror going for another few years, I could visualize myself staying in Centre County and actually getting a college degree (and then what ... teaching?) instead of wandering off to pursue that goal of working for a major metro.

But it all works out in the end, doesn't it? Even if the reason for my going to The Mirror remains obscure to me (don't we hate to admit we did things on a whim?) I have never regretted it for a moment. I became part of a really talented group of people working for an editor, Dave Fay, who was sometimes wild and rowdy but he was our leader.

But mostly, I've never regretted it because working at The Mirror was just a ton of fun.

French-cut green beans!

CHAPTER 9
LIGHTS OUT FOR HOY BROTHERS STORE

By Bill Welch

(Bill Welch, who rose to executive editor of the Centre Daily Times, earned a reputation as a first-rate writer. This story on the closing of Hoy Brothers store, from May 5, 1973, is an example of his talent.)

SHARP EYE FOR DETAIL – CDT editor Bill Welch didn't write often but when he did, people took notice. (Photo courtesy of Tom Berner)

On May 4 of this year, for the first time in 40 years, they turned on all the lights at the Hoy Brothers' store in State College. The next day they went out for the last time, at the close of a two-day auction.

There's a story about those lights. Hoy Brothers seemed to deal in stories as much as anything else.

At the auction, one store patron recalled some of them.

He first passed through those double swinging doors in 1947. He was six years old and his dad had moved his offices into the house next door. The high point of the youngster's week was a Saturday morning visit to his father's office. But the real goal of those visits was next door.

That was how it started, with a taste for Cokes and Pepsis mixed by hand, with lemon or vanilla or cherry syrup added; with salt-crusted pretzels and ice cream made right there in the store.

But there was more, and mostly it was the stories. Stories by the Hoy brothers and about them and stories swapped by customers loafing away an afternoon, lingering for a second soda and then a third.

It was Dick and Jim Hoy reminiscing about their boyhood in Waddle, where their father was stationmaster on the Bellefonte Central Railroad, and postmaster and storekeeper and just about everything there was to be in Waddle at the turn of the century. Stories about their mother baking bread in a round pan lined with cabbage leaves, which yielded a veined loaf. Stories about skinny-dipping in view of the passengers on trains rounding the Little Horseshoe Curve at Waddle, carrying students to the college, which the Hoys would eventually attend, graduating in 1924 and 1932 and opening their store in the depths of the Depression.

It was Dick – bow-tied, talkative – telling about the Armistice Day parade in which Jim played Kaiser Bill, or about the summer of 1927 or 1928 when he and Jim drove from State College to Cuba,[13] and visited a moonshiner in Virginia and were peppered by mosquitoes in untamed Florida.

It was Jim – older, quieter – making notes in the Farmer's Almanac, keeping them and comparing today's snowstorm with the one 10 years ago, and recalling how they'd had to get up on the roof of the store one year and shovel the snow off to keep it from collapsing.

The youngster remembers sitting in the store on muggy summer afternoons, waiting for the thunderclouds to roll in from the west, from behind the University Club across the street, and when they'd arrive, the winds would push the swinging doors open, just like the Invisible Man had walked in.

Hoy Brothers was pinball games (with a tournament at Easter, when the youngster and his friends were older and some were home from college for the holidays); reading comic books and then magazines, True, Argosy, Men's Adventure and Playboy, but

---

13 Probably Cuba Mills, an unincorporated patch in Juniata County.

also Harper's and Atlantic Monthly. It was discovering that Theodore Roethke, the poet, loafed at Hoys when he lived at the University Club.

It was chocolate milk, with chocolate syrup made in the store, from a recipe Dick wouldn't reveal. It was the Artic-Aire floor fan humming at the summer heat. It was the Cokes for a nickel, then for seven cents, 10 centers, 12 cents, always the last place in town to raise the price.

It was a laundry delivery man who had served with Patton; a University professor who arrived at the same time every day for years, and had the same milk shake and crackers for lunch; boys who became bankers, astronomers, teachers and some who never seemed to become anything.

It was this story, which may or may not be true, but which tells a lot about the way their customers viewed the Hoy Brothers and why they felt about them the way they did:

Twenty years ago, Hoy Brothers was the only store in town to stock those small, four-wheeled dollies which restaurants put their garbage cans on so they can be rolled, not lugged, from place to place. They were a popular item and many restaurant owners bought them. One man bought several, and liked them.

He approached Dick about buying a dozen more and praised their usefulness.

"We quit carrying them," Dick said. "There got to be too many people in here bothering us for them."

Hoy Brothers may have been the only store in town which closed down for three weeks every year, so the owners could go on vacation. There weren't any employees to take over, just Dick and Jim, so they'd close the store for the three weeks before Labor Day.

The Hoy Brothers, at one time or another, sold pants, coats, spats, greeting cards, bottled gas, appliances, groceries, shirts and a hundred other items. For a while they rented tuxedos, which explains where the lone fancy vest came from which they auctioned off last May. The auction crew turned up some unexpected items

– a massive cider press in the basement, a fencing mask, and a box of tennis balls.

The store's lights, actually its dim lighting, was almost its trademark. It certainly was to those who'd say: "Oh, it's so gloomy, I'd never go in there" or "You mean that dark store up past Sears?"[14] Those were customers the Hoys didn't need. Let them go to the stores with fluorescent lights and tile floors and spare them the oiled wooden floors and the globe lights hanging from the ceiling. They couldn't appreciate the simple thrift of not turning on the lights where you aren't.

At Hoy's, a customer was an event and a purchase a mild surprise.

But there was always something of a rush at Christmastime and the store was open every evening and Dick hung greens from the cords of the ceiling lights. One year the youngster's aunt bought him a Hoy Brothers credit card – an index card which Jim typed up to resemble a meal ticket. It could get you a Coke when your allowance ran out.

Christmas each year brought one of the best Hoy traditions – a Christmas party. (There were others, like guessing which day Jim would finally decide it was safe to put up the screen doors; it was usually the middle of June.)

On Christmas Eve, the store would close at 5 o'clock and for an hour or two the Hoy Brothers and their favorite customers were just the Hoy Brothers with their friends. There weren't any formal invitations; you knew whether you were welcome or not. Dick would show color slides he took at a beer party the youngster and his friends had in a mountain meadow one Easter in lieu of the pinball tournament. One Christmas, Jim bought beer, and let it chill in the snow on the back porch. The youngster thought it was the best beer he ever drank.

The hours, the years at Hoys, were among the youngster's, and the man's, happiest. That happiness is fading. Dick had to retire from an active part in the business a few years ago because of his

---

14 Sears was located at 232 West College Avenue. Today it is a Starbucks. Hoy Brothers was at 324 West College. The building—and others with it—were razed for an apartment complex.

health. Jim kept the store open by himself, working long hours, cutting back where he could, on doctor's orders. First the groceries went, then the fountain was closed to all but the favorite customers. And finally the fountain failed, for lack of a repair part which could not be found.

The last time the youngster saw Jim Hoy was on a winter morning. He stopped in the store and asked Jim, who was bundled up against the cold and drafts, when the fountain might be repaired.

"Junior," he said (he always called me Junior), "you've had your last Hoy Brothers Pepsi." He died a few days later. Two days after the auction, Dick also died.

The dark green counter, the stools, the racks and stands and cases that were Hoy Brothers General Merchandise Store are scattered now. But for some of us, it will always be Easter or Christmas in the middle of June.

CHAPTER 10
SO THIS IS JOURNALISM?

By Gary Tuma

An essay for *Esquire Magazine* in 1977 by Harry Crews contained this passage:

> "All of us whose senses are not entirely dead realize the imperfections of what we do, and to the extent that we are hard on ourselves, that imperfection translates itself into failure."

Is the protagonist of the tale that follows hard on himself? He certainly prefers to avoid these walks down memory lane, conjur-

MOVING ON UP – Gary Tuma, left, started out as a Centre Daily Times sportswriter and ended his working career as press secretary for Pennsylvania Governor Ed Rendell. (Photo courtesy of Gary Tuma)

ing up as they do a vast mental litany of his own shortcomings and fuck-ups. He would rather just live life today as he finds it, but reminiscence now of those three years at the Centre Daily Times seems to be more from another world than from another era, so he's making an exception.

This tale of imperfection is a window on that world, but who knows how clear or foggy. Is it likewise a tale of failure? The protagonist might have an opinion, but you can decide.

***

Joe Paterno was trying mightily to put on his pants, but he wasn't having much luck. He had one leg in, but he was hopping around dragging the other pant leg across the floor of his office while changing clothes at the Penn State football practice facility. The distraction was me. He was waving his free arm – the one not clutching his pants—and screaming: "Get outta here!"

Fresh out of Penn State in the autumn of 1974, I was a few months into my first newspaper job at the Centre Daily Times, known colloquially as the CDT.

Penn State's sports information office had issued a short press release about a newly hired assistant coach, which was unusual for mid-season, unusual because there was no staff vacancy, and unusual for the minimal description of his duties.

My boss, assistant sports editor Ron Bracken, told me to get more info from Joe after practice, so we could do a nice feature story on the new coach. I went to Paterno's office after practice and innocently asked about the unconventional hire.

Paterno went berserk. He shouted at the top of his voice. "So we hired a guy," he yelled. "Whaddya coming around here for asking these questions. Get outta here."

I stood motionless for a moment, thinking he must have misunderstood my simple inquiry. My mouth was open but nothing came out. He kept hollering at me ... "I don't have time for these questions!"

Half shocked and half mystified, I left. I went back to the office with no story about the new assistant coach.

So this was journalism, eh?

How did I end up here, a 22-year-old kid, in the locker room office of an already-legendary head coach who was inexplicably pissed off at me?

I had never been much interested in being a newspaper reporter. I started my freshman year at Penn State as a psychology major, but that involved a little too much boring scientific method, and it turned out the stuff I wrote for my basic English classes was reasonably good. I always loved to read. So I became an English major with a writing emphasis. No mere journalism school for me. As a future great American novelist, I preferred a more literary approach.

By my senior year I was doing well enough that Professor Philip Klass, the English Department's internship coordinator, proposed me for one of the writing program's three internships in winter term. One of those was at the CDT. Another was at a publishing company that produced several airline in-flight magazines, and the third was at "Penthouse" magazine.

The magazines sounded a lot more prestigious and more aligned with my writing interests, but Klass told me my style suited newspaper work – quite a comedown for a future great American novelist. Still, it was nine credits without going to class, so I took it.

To digress for a moment, my path would cross both airline magazines and "Penthouse" a few years later, in much different contexts.

While working for a South Florida newspaper in the late 1970s, I discovered that a Miami-based company published the in-flight magazine for a major U.S. airline. I dropped in on the editor, and landed a freelance gig for a few years writing articles for magazines that, as I heard in a line from a movie once, they put in the seat pocket, right next to the barf bags.

As for "Penthouse," I found myself playing one night in a charity softball game on a team of South Florida sports media "celebrities" against a team of Penthouse Pets, the equivalent of the Playboy centerfolds. It occurred at decrepit old Miami Stadium, where the Class A affiliate of the Baltimore Orioles used to play its Florida State League home games.

I also played on a rec league softball team at the time, so my batting stroke was tuned up. On my first plate appearance, I scorched a line drive through the right side of the infield. It rolled toward one of the Pets playing the outfield. Suspecting that her throwing arm was not her chief physical attribute, I hustled around first and stretched it into a double. The umpire for the night – an actual celebrity Gold-Glove-winning former major leaguer of Latin American descent — approached me. Expecting him to say something like "nice hit," I instead saw him glaring at me.

"Are you crazy?" he said. "What are you doing hitting a ball that hard in a game like this. Are you trying to kill one of these little girls?" He walked away from me contemptuously.

"Little girls?" I recall wondering to myself.

But back to my CDT internship. At first I was assigned a few features or simple inside-page short news stories. Then America started running out of gas, lucky for me. One morning in early 1974 the city editor, Tom Berner, handed me an assignment. There were rumors of an impending gasoline shortage. No one knew quite how seriously to take it, so Berner told me to make a few calls. I started contacting gas stations in and around State College and — Wow! — owners told me they expected to be out of supply by tonight, tomorrow, or whenever, but very soon.

I had a front-page story. Soon a major gas crisis gripped the nation. Lines at service stations stretched for blocks. People were afraid to take long trips. It was big news for weeks, but the CDT kept little intern me on the gas beat from the ground floor up, and I stayed on the front page.

Around the office, I often talked sports with other reporters. Seeing my interest, the CDT offered me $25 per game to cover high school basketball in the evening after my unpaid daytime internship. When I was ready to graduate, they said they had been considering expanding their sports department (then two full-time writers) and asked if I would like to join the staff. So I was employed right out of college without the angst of job applications. I earned something like $140 per week, pathetic even then. When I told my dad, who had paid part of my Penn State tuition, he looked at me dumbfounded. "I didn't think anyone paid that low anymore," he said. (Editor's note: The Pa. Mirror paid lower!)

I had been a CDT regular staffer just a few days in the summer of 1974 when two young fellows came into the office to promote the fairly new sport of hang gliding. They had a proposition: If the paper was interested, they would do a demonstration and even let a reporter give it a try.

The next day, guinea pig I and photographer Dick Brown met them at the top of a local ski slope that was closed for summer. They gave me a little background on the history and physics of the sport, and showed me how to control the kite. Then one of the guys strapped himself in, took a running start, and went soaring into the air hundreds of feet above the ski slope.

Brown, who was a licensed small plane pilot, looked at me and laughed. "I've been up in all kinds of aircraft," he said, "but you couldn't get me to do that for a million dollars."

Nonetheless, a few minutes later I was strapped into the kite. I'm still alive today because we did not start at the top of the mountain, but rather closer to the bottom. I got my running start, went up in the air maybe 15 feet, then lost control and careened into the ground. A few bruises, nothing serious, but that was the end of my kamikaze mission for the day.

Another fine summer day was wasted when the CDT sent me to a local country club to cover its golf championship. I guess the owners of the paper were members. I spent an otherwise nice Sunday trailing some businessman types around the course with their friends and family, then writing a story, as if anyone gave a rat's ass. That came back to haunt me a few months later.

The fall weekend life of most State College sportswriters at the time entailed high school football on a Friday night, drinking at bars afterward, then getting up in time – meaning about 10:30 a.m. – to make it to the press box in time for the Nittany Lions' Saturday kickoff.

But bright and early (like 7 a.m.) on one Saturday morning, hung over and halfway into what should have been my night's sleep, I answered the ringing phone in my apartment. On the other end was the wife of one of the businessman golfers who had walked around the country-club course with me that afternoon. She informed me that Arnold Palmer was flying in with her husband (whose company had some kind of business relationship with the famed golfer) for the Penn State-Wake Forest game that afternoon. Arnie was a Wake Forest grad. She was letting me know so I could meet them when they landed at the airport, and get a "scoop."

She meant well, but the last thing I wanted to do was roll out of bed at that hour and go to the airport to do an interview for which I had done zero preparation. I showered, dressed, and red-eyed and disheveled, met them when they landed. What kinds of questions did I have? Well, I couldn't really think of any good ones. What brings you to town? We already knew that. Do you go to a lot of Wake Forest games? Who cares? Prediction on who will win? Lame.

The execs and a wife or two stood there on the tarmac, hoping for an inside look at an actual reporter interviewing an actual sports superstar. Instead they witnessed a half-asleep, hungover refugee from Friday night high school football and bar-hopping bumble through what barely approximated a coherent conversation – and witnessed an increasingly annoyed but ever-polite Arnie manifest an expression that conveyed a question of his own: Who is this jerk?

Thanks to the tip from the wife, however, I did indeed have an exclusive interview with Arnie, although to this day I still doubt it was worth the embarrassment.

Penn State was invited to the Cotton Bowl at the end of that 1974 season for an unglamorous match-up against Baylor. The two veterans on the staff, Bracken and Doug McDonald, decided they would let the rookie reporter cover the bowl game. Big mistake.

For a month between the invitation and the trip to Dallas, I listened to Brown, the CDT star photographer, bad-mouth Bracken's and McDonald's bowl trip stories of prior years. They write stories based on those dry routine press conferences and never capture the flavor of the thing, he told me repeatedly. Although Bracken mentioned in passing once that I should be careful about taking Brown's advice too seriously, I went to Dallas determined to write fresh, colorful stories, rather than work off the same stale press conference interviews as other reporters. Accordingly, I skipped those canned press events. But since practices were closed and there was no other access to the players and coaches, I had no material to write about. The result was the worst newspaper coverage of a major bowl in the annals of college football. I might still hold the record.

***

Most small and medium-sized towns in America had one newspaper then. While State College was blessed with two, those of us at the CDT considered the upstart Pennsylvania Mirror a curse. The CDT was a long-time Centre County institution. The Mirror was a young intruder into the market. So we had competition, which is good for the community but a pain in the ass for the reporter. Especially in our case, because that competition was strong. The Mirror had a lively sports section thanks to some excellent writers and reporters, and a certain devil-may-care attitude that was out-of-place at the staid old CDT. Mirror sports editor Terry Nau set the tone with an approach that was loose and carefree, yet was combined with a journalistic drive to get the story first, and produce a good sports section.

Both sports departments had their wins and losses. Our sports editor, Bracken, was an excellent columnist and was well plugged in to the local sports scene and broke a lot of stories. For me, though, the losses tended to stick with me. The many occasions when the

Mirror guys did a better job bothered me, but it was probably good for me. I spent about 15 more years as a reporter after I left the CDT, almost all of it up against better reporters who, as the old Mike Lange line about hockey goaltenders goes, beat me like a rented mule. So my CDT experience was a character builder.

There was one area where the CDT had it over the Mirror, though. Our paper actually made money — not that much of it found its way to my wallet.

We did have our moments of fun at the CDT, though, like the time Bracken and I wrote a column that actually ran in the competition. Mirror sportswriter Dennis Gildea used to write a funny and irreverent weekly football prediction column under the pseudonym of T. Wes Brillik, accompanied by a cartoon logo of a grizzly, bearded thug-like character. One time, Bracken and I decided to spoof it. We wrote an outrageous take-off predicting that weekend's games. I showed it to Nau, who showed it to Gildea, who said: Hey, that's good enough for me, I can take this week off. So the Mirror printed it under the Brillik byline. That our work was a parody of Gildea's column didn't bother them, since Gildea's work was itself a parody of conventional prediction columns.

For some strange reason, Bracken confessed to the powers that be at the CDT that we had written the Mirror prediction column that week. They were not happy, but there was no retribution, other than Bracken being subjected to some hostile eye-rolling.

I had some laughs at the expense of the Mirror once. A prominent State College bar owner (Jack Sapia), whose establishment we often hung out at, had conceived an allegedly brilliant idea to raise money for Penn State athletics. The university would "sell" small pieces (a square foot, if I recall) of the Beaver Stadium field. Purchasers would get a certificate testifying that they "owned" a part of the hallowed Nittany Lions' playing surface. He proposed this in an interview with a Mirror reporter, Dennis Gildea, who wrote a column.

The light bulb went off in my head when I read it. I wrote a satirical response in the CDT, noting that there wasn't much anyone could do with a square foot of earth, so why not sell something more utilitarian, like six-foot sections that could be used as grave plots. I laid out an entire argument, with reasons such as surviving family members who hold season tickets being able to visit their loved one's grave six or seven times a year while they cheer on Dear Old State, and the well maintained sod getting better care than the lawn at the average cemetery.

Other than a few more literal readers who didn't get the joke and called the CDT to complain that it was a dumb idea, most people, even Mirror sportswriters, thought it was hilarious. I guess you had to be there.

But it did quickly put the nail in the coffin, so to speak, of the bar owner's proposal. The idea was never heard from again.

As these anecdotes suggest, Mirror and CDT sportswriters knew each other well. It was inevitable – small sports writing staffs, continually interacting as we covered the same events in a small town, and drinking together in bars afterword, which is pretty much all there was to do for predominantly single guys who typically quit working late at night.

So we were all friends, or at any rate people who spent a lot of time together. I think it's fair to say the CDT sports staff and my competitors on the Mirror sports section felt more like my co-workers than did staffers from other departments at the CDT.

This eventually progressed to the extreme when Nau and I ended up sharing the same three-bedroom rental house. I had originally leased it with two other guys, but in a college town, young single people come and go. They moved out, others moved in, and eventually Nau was looking for a new place around the same time we had a vacant bedroom.

At first it was an ordinary domicile on Old Boalsburg Road in a suburban-style State College neighborhood, but when Nau moved in, that changed everything.

About every three months, roughly quarterly —spring, summer, fall, winter – we would throw a party at the house. When I say "we," well, all three pitched in to do the work, but the impetus came from Terry. Usually, there would be more than a hundred people, jammed into this little white wooden frame house, and spilling out into the yard. Multiple kegs of beer. Everything from young recent Penn State grads to older married couples. You never knew who would be there. At one party, Steelers running back Franco Harris left a cigarette burn mark on the old family wooden coffee table that my mother gave me when I was furnishing the house. It didn't matter all that much because another time, former Penn State wrestler and Mirror sportswriter Chris Koll broke a leg off the table while horsing around in our living room.

Once, I invited friends from Pittsburgh to visit on one of our party weekends. Five of them came, one with his little suburbanite wife along. When the party wound down sometime in the middle of the night, one of them got a broom to clear away the crunched Cheetos and potato chips from a spot on the living room carpet to lie down and sleep. Do I know how to treat guests, or what? One of them admitted to me a few years later that they didn't have a good time.

At one party on a rainy fall night, the dozens of attendees had tracked wet leaves all through the house. J.D. Andrews, a Mirror sportswriter, arrived. He walked in, looked at the leaf-strewn floor and deadpanned, "I love your autumn décor."

The parties eventually became pretty famous around town. One prime example: Two days before one of our legendary shindigs, a few of us were at the Shandygaff Saloon, which was always packed for Thursday oldies night. We struck up a conversation with a couple girls whom we had never seen nor met before. After a while, they seemed cool enough, so Terry told them we were having a party at our house on Saturday, and invited them. They said they were already planning to go to a party on Saturday, but asked for our address. If the other party was a bore, they would switch to ours. We gave them our address and they looked at us with puzzlement. "That's the party we're already invited to," one of them said. We had no idea who they were.

Looking back, it was kind of amazing that we didn't do major damage to the house. A former Penn State linebacker once got some carrots from our fridge, half chewed them, and spit out the pieces all over the kitchen. One of our friends had a worse experience. He held a party at his house where one of our crowd, finding the bathroom occupied, pissed on the carpet in the corner of the living room. At least that never happened to us. I don't think it did, anyway.

But it wasn't full-time bacchanalia at our house. We were a group with an interest in quality journalism and quality writing. We had quite a few conversations about the best work being done by sportswriters round the country, and about other fine writing as well.

***

So on we went, covering high schools and Penn State sports. I was the beat man on a Nittany Lions sport each season – soccer in the fall, basketball in the winter, lacrosse in the spring. Almost always there was a Mirror reporter there too, and often, after going to our respective offices to write our stories, we gathered again at the bars till closing time, or at somebody's house.

Hanging over everything, of course, was football. It was the major subject of interest in Centre County, and in a sense it was never out of season. It pervaded everything. All three full-time sportswriters at the CDT covered home games and road games within driving distance. One would go on the flying trips. The Mirror operated similarly.

When I left half-dressed Paterno's office that evening in the middle of my first season, after his blow-up at me over the hiring of the new assistant coach, I figured it had defined our relationship for good. As far as I knew, he would be my enemy from then on. I had no use for him. But the next time I saw him, in a post-game interview, he was cordial and cooperative. It was the first sign for me that a sportswriter never knew quite what to expect. No matter what sort of unpleasantness you encounter, you have to go back again and cover what you are assigned to cover if you are going to remain in the business. I covered PSU football for three seasons, with no other major incidents with Paterno.

I would find out later that the new assistant coach was hired mainly to handle recruiting. Back then, Paterno, as well as most coaches at other schools, were paranoid about high school recruiting news. It was all hush-hush, not like now, when high school stars' college announcements are treated like the Oscars. No, Paterno freaked out at me because he didn't want any stories in the paper that had anything whatsoever to do with recruiting. Part of that was him not wanting to tip off other schools on recruits he was courting, but I also believe in a way he was trying to protect those young kids from the media spotlight. Well into his career, for example, he wouldn't let freshmen, and for a time not even sophomores, talk to the press.

I would wonder years later if I had seen then the seeds of an attitude that would cause so much trouble. Protecting players and protecting the football program intersected somewhere with reflexive secretiveness, and the fulcrum had to be in just the right place to achieve proper balance. Whoever bears the blame, it wasn't. I would wonder if the intense desire to keep parts of the program hidden from public view had become so habitual that it partly contributed to such terrible consequences for some young children, for the university, and for Paterno himself three and a half decades on.

There was much more in the shadows. There always is, and not all of it dark. One night in the summer of 1975, Bracken, McDonald and I covered the Big 33, then a major high school football all-star game played in Hershey. Most of the Penn State coaching staff usually attended. This year, though, the assistants were proceeding on to a wedding, so the Penn State sports information office asked if we could give Paterno a lift back to State College.

I sat in the middle of the back seat, Paterno to my right and Bracken to my left. As we began to talk, I sensed an uncomfortable predicament. We were not gathered for an interview; we were just hauling him home. Would his utterances be fair game for inclusion in an article, or did he assume the conversation was private. I decided to confront the quandary head on.

"Joe, be sure to let us know what is on the record and what is off," I said.

"Whaddya mean?" he said. "Everything we say tonight is off the record."

Bracken told me later he was relieved that I had clarified the matter, because he was sitting beside me wondering if Paterno's utterances might be column fodder.

So we had a normal conversation. Paterno expressed opinions freely, as if he were with a bunch of guys watching a game in the basement over wings and beer. He spoke of college and pro players, of other coaches, of the state of college football, of education.

For much of what he said, I admired him. I had written a column a few weeks earlier about youth baseball. This was in the day before most leagues had rules requiring players to get into the game for a few innings and bat at least once. I said it was wrong that youth programs occupied young kids' time and then let them do nothing but sit on the bench.

"Gary, I almost wrote you a letter a while back," Paterno said at one point. He strongly agreed with the column, adding that perhaps adults generally tended to over-organize kids' games, placing too much pressure on children at a time when they should be just playing to have fun. He told a story of seeing a group of boys coming door to door down his street. When they reached his house, he greeted them and they asked him for a donation for their baseball team. He said no. The boys were momentarily confused, not sure if he was kidding, then Paterno pointed to the two cars in his driveway. "But if you wash those cars for me I'll give you each five dollars," he told them. They said they didn't have time and went back to the street. A father who had waited at the curb came forward and asked if there was a problem. "Yes," Paterno told him. "You're teaching these kids to be beggars."

I interviewed Paterno many times over the years, wrote feature articles on him, and attended maybe a hundred press conferences with him. I never learned quite as much about the real Paterno in those interviews as I did that night. I read many profiles of him in newspapers and magazines since then, including some by damn good writers. Somehow though, they never quite captured the man I was with on that car ride, when he spoke openly, knowing that what he said would not show up in the paper. I never quite captured him in print either. The best story I might ever have written about Joe Paterno, I was constrained from writing. I would still be honoring his off-the-record request today if he were alive.

Some years later, when I was a state political reporter for the Pittsburgh Post-Gazette, I gave a lift to a nationally known celebrity who had endorsed a candidate at a press conference in Philadelphia, then had to give a speech that night in Harrisburg. She made a perfunctory comment or two in the first few minutes, then said: "If I fall asleep, don't feel bad. The riding makes me drowsy." Sure enough, she closed her eyes, and I chauffeured her silently for the next two hours.

No story there, either.

When reporters are in their official roles, their access to prominent people often produces a distorted image, precisely because of who and what reporters are. Ideally, the reporter is a sort of Everyman-With-Notebook, but in fact, filters intrude between journalists and reality, and they see only warped semblances. It's not just the spin doctors and imagine makers, or the lies. There are more subtle factors, too. People in the public eye become media savvy, and perceive beforehand how their statements will appear in print. They eventually learn that even fair reporters might be pitiless in using any detail at their disposal. Show something of your true inner self and the reporter will steal it for his own purposes. So they give stock answers, and interviews become more recitations than conversation. A Paterno stays off the record with familiar reporters; a celebrity sleeps, or pretends to, while traveling with a reporter she doesn't know if she can trust. Who can blame her for not wanting some guy to interpret her for the public on the basis of a two-hour car trip?

I conscientiously endeavored to be accurate, but inevitably I painted imperfect pictures. I revealed some things, omitted others, and didn't manage even a glimpse of most. I wrote stories pretending to explain people soaring over mountains while I barely got off the ground near the bottom of the slope, then crashed.

In his 1974 best-selling novel "Zen and the Art of Motorcycle Maintenance," Robert Pirsig wrote: "We take a handful of sand from the endless landscape of awareness around us and call that handful of sand the world."

How much does it matter?

For a while I was all about journalism *verité*, until the notion slowly crept into my brain, then took it over like a virus: the public doesn't want truthfulness, it wants entertainment, and it wants to believe what it wants to believe, facts be damned. God bless reporters who still care.

I know this much now. A real reporter on that day in the fall of 1974 would have dug deeper to find out about Paterno's new hire. He would have written about Paterno blowing his top when asked about it, and would have been suspicious because a simple and perfectly predictable question about a new coach had provoked such an intense reaction. But I was not a real reporter. Not then, maybe not ever.

***

Without another job, I quit the CDT in 1977. The city boy didn't want to live in the sleepy hamlet of State College anymore. I moved back home to Pittsburgh, where I spent the next 18 months mostly unemployed, living with my dad. And he thought I was lowly paid at the CDT. Hah! I managed to pick up some stringing work for the Pittsburgh Post-Gazette, covering high school games — almost back where I started at the CDT.

Finally, while helping a friend move to Florida, I dropped off an application at a paper in the Miami suburb of Hollywood.

They had an opening, so I got a job. It was not fortunate timing; they almost always had openings in the sports department, because reporters couldn't bear to stay there. It was the most miserable place I ever worked, for the most awful boss. I covered the Miami Dolphins and a half dozen other things each of my typical 14-hour days. And it was there in Florida that I would smack a solid line drive through a bevy of Pets, thus bringing derision upon myself from someone who had actually made a living playing baseball.

After a tortuous year and a half, I returned to the Post-Gazette as a full-time staffer. Within two years I was promoted to beat man covering the Pittsburgh Steelers. Within two more years I was demoted to covering the rest of the National Football League, along with a couple of things called the Major Indoor Soccer League and Arena Football.

Since I was struggling so badly as a sportswriter, the Post-Gazette assigned me something a lot easier: covering state government.

Three and a half years into my time at the Harrisburg bureau, I was laid off because a Teamsters Union strike shut down the Pittsburgh papers. Five months later I took a job as press secretary at the Department of Education. With me in charge of messaging, a controversial major education reform proposal bit the dust. When the Casey Administration changed to the Ridge Administration, I was fired. I then worked for a state Senator and a state Treasurer, who did some good things for the people of Pennsylvania —until they got indicted. In between, I became the third of three press secretaries for Governor Ed Rendell, who had won reelection in a landslide (before I became his P.R. guy) but after making some difficult decisions to deal with the Great Recession, ended his tenure with horrible approval numbers (with me as his P.R. guy.) I eventually became press secretary to a lieutenant governor, who lost his reelection bid in the primary, but by then I had already retired. Now I collect Social Security and two pension checks while my wonderful wife of 20 years —I got that right, but it took two tries – and I do yard work and walk our beagle. I've never had any kind of social media account. Professionally, I do what Jack Nicholson's character in the classic 1974 movie "Chinatown" wisely advised: "As little as possible," present chapter of this book excepted.

***

When he was city editor, Berner had a Plexiglas shield over his desk, under which he kept various notes, pictures, reminders, and so forth. On one scrap of paper was a quotation from John Updike's 1970 work "Bech, A Book." It read: "Actuality is a running impoverishment of possibility."

Perhaps that realization is the inescapable yardstick by which we measure imperfection against failure. The protagonist is 67 now, but his senses are more entirely alive than ever, and he alone will decide how hard to be on himself. Your opinion doesn't matter much.

CHAPTER 11
MY FAVORITE YEAR

By Glenn Sheeley

There was no other year like it in my life. Thrown in with a crazy bunch of people, doing what we all loved, which was to fill a newspaper every night (and I mean, fill it, since there were hardly any ads), race to a favorite bar immediately after deadline, smoke too much, consume too many beers and then sleep until noon. Then do it all over again the next day.

After impersonating a student for four years at Penn State and spending 90 percent of my time at The Daily Collegian, now this was more like it. In the shadow of the Penn State campus, still writing about Joe Paterno's world but now with a little cash in my pocket and no classes to attend, what could be better?

HAPPILY RETIRED – Glenn Sheeley, former Mirror sportswriter, shown here with grandson Tyler, worked in Pittsburgh and Atlanta after leaving State College. (Photo by Jessica Reupert)

I think I was making 110 bucks a week at the Pennsylvania Mirror and I can never remember hurting for cash. Of course, it helped that draft beers were maybe 50 cents and a Cheese Whopper cost less than a buck.

I had called Terry Nau in August of 1973 after the job I had taken with the Orlando Sentinel's Brevard County Bureau in Cocoa, Fla. turned out to offer sunshine, a nearby beach and little else.

"No, I don't want a camera," I told the managing editor, "and I don't take pictures."

He accused me of merely taking the job as summer employment, with no intention to remain full-time, and said I was fired.

"Everything I own was in this car when I came down here," I said. "You can't fire me. I quit."

Come work for me at the Mirror, Terry said. I was just in time for football season, which started in a couple of weeks with a road game at Stanford, and he needed help covering the Nittany Lions while also putting out the paper every night.

Sign me up. I'm there. I cleaned out my Cape Canaveral Beach studio apartment, loaded up my new AMC Hornet (a putrid, yellowish-orange color, but the only one on the lot with AC for summer in Florida) and headed back to State College.

Best decision I ever made. Good thing, too, because my only other employment possibility then was a P.R. gig with the Space Coast Golf Tour in Cocoa Beach, which sounded a helluva lot better than it actually was. It died way before the Mirror did.

***

Terry and I had spent a couple of fun years together at The Collegian, where he eventually became sports editor and I moved from reporter to assistant sports editor. When he graduated in 1972, I took over the head position. We covered a lot of Penn State football together as students, working and playing hard, and establishing ourselves firmly as a persistent, often irreverent check on Penn State athletics.

Although we both had decent relationships with Paterno and he respected our roles, even as students, still present was nearly every coach's perception that we should help the team, rather than write "negative" stories. Of course, we hoped Penn State won – it made the school's reputation soar and increased its national presence – but it wasn't really necessary.

For instance, when I was a student at the Collegian and the Lions were having fumble problems one year, I ran a mug shot of a "turnover" in the paper (a blurred, bouncing football) and before long there were references to "Joe Paternover."

Joe was pretty pissed at that.

`On the other hand, in 1973 when I was exiting the Collegian as sports editor, which you were required to do in the spring term of your senior year, we ran a satirical story about me "Leaving Penn State for the Money," a takeoff on Joe's decision in January to turn down a million-dollar offer from the NFL's New England Patriots.

Joe even had a good laugh at that story, as I understood, but he never admitted as much to me.

(On a personal note, it probably saved my Journalism degree, too. Turns out my professors liked the story, which took up almost the entire front page, enough to forget that I had barely done much else for them the entire spring trimester. Happily, they knew the experience I was getting at the Collegian was more valuable than reading about Marshall McLuhan.)

People in the PSU Athletic Department seemed to forget the times in which we were immersed back then. Watergate was happening before our eyes. Every journalist was inspired by what The Washington Post was able to do – expose the wrongdoings of a President and force his eventual resignation.

Plus, the Vietnam War was raging in the late 60s's and early 70's and, as every journalist discovered, the Nixon administration had regularly lied to the American people regarding the conflict. Imagine if the press had not been there to hold the government accountable! This was the exact moment in history when we were enrolled in Journalism classes (even attending some of them) and positioning ourselves to work for newspapers as professionals. With that in mind, it was pretty easy to maintain one's objectivity to cover a sports team – even your own college.

Unfortunately, most athletes never seemed to get our relationship, either. A few years later, when I was covering the Steelers for The Pittsburgh Press in the mid-1970's, I remember Franco Harris, a fellow Penn Stater, looking over at me from a training room table after a rare loss and saying, "You know, we're all in this together, Glenn, right?"

Actually, Franco, uh, no. Not even close.

As an experience, yes. But hardly with the same goals. I got paid the same whether a team I was covering won or lost. My responsibility was to management and my editors. And to my own pride and reputation.

Undoubtedly, both the Collegian and the Mirror were incredible preparations for my five years with The Pittsburgh Press and then beyond, for what evolved as a 26-year career with the Atlanta Journal-Constitution, covering the NFL and other pro sports, and then golf from 1994 to 2005.

Talk about an impressive trifecta of subjects to cover from college to the end of my newspaper career:

– Penn State's 31-game unbeaten streak in the late 1960's.

– The Steelers' ascension to Super Bowl champions after 39 years of misery.

– The rise of Tiger Woods to arguably the best player in golf history (although I still lean toward Jack Nicklaus).

In all, I was fortunate to cover 17 Super Bowls, 21 Masters, 17 US Opens, eight British Opens, a few Ryder Cups and some NLCS and World Series games in the mid-90's. From 1998 to 2005, I covered 32 straight major golf championships, including 10 of Tiger's major wins.

But I can honestly say I worked just as hard at, say, a Penn State basketball game as I did covering a Super Bowl or Masters. The pride factor is the same whether it's a couple hundred people reading your story or a few million. Either way, you can still wake up sweating in the middle of the night, wondering if you spelled a name correctly or messed up a statistic. You didn't get any do-overs in a newspaper. It was right there for everyone to see in the morning.

***

The Collegian was given away for free, but it had a 30,000 circulation, triple that of the Mirror, and was quite a legit daily paper. We published Tuesday-Saturday and ran national stories along with the University and State College news. We competed with both the Mirror and the Centre Daily Times and we worked long hours.

During football season, we were at it seven days a week, and for little more than beer money. The sports editor got a stipend of $35 a week. The assistant sports editor made $22.50. Senior reporters got 10 bucks a week. But we loved it, and we dreamed daily about doing this for a living, without the burden of school, and making a decent income.

We broke stories, occasionally some with national impact. I ran into Steve Joachim, a highly-touted Penn State quarterback prospect, in the Lion's Den one Friday night and he told me he was transferring to Temple. I called him back in the morning, with a clearer head, and he confirmed. Thank goodness, nobody else got wind of it and we were able to break it in Tuesday's Collegian, from where it was picked up by the Associated Press and distributed nationwide.

At the Mirror, I broke the story that Penn State's John Cappelletti, the 1973 Heisman Trophy winner, was to dedicate the trophy to his little brother, Joey, who was suffering from leukemia. Though tiny, the Mirror had enough credibility that a story appearing on our pages would be distributed aggressively by the wire services.

Funny, whenever I think about John Cappelletti, the first thing I always think of has nothing to with the unique fluidity and relentlessness of his running style. It's of his early years, when he was initially placed at defensive back due to a temporary surplus at running back with a couple of guys named Franco Harris and Lydell Mitchell.

After a mid-week practice, I was scanning the locker room for interviews and came upon Cappy standing with a couple of other defensive backs. In mid-question, I was interrupted by Paterno, who said, "Don't ask these guys any questions, Glenn. They're freshmen. They don't know anything."

Well, somebody must have known something. A few years later, Joe was standing with Cappelletti holding the Heisman Trophy, flanked by none other than Bob Hope.

The relationship I developed both at the Collegian and the Mirror with some of the country's finest sportswriters, especially the Northeastern guys, was immeasurably valuable. Penn State was a prime beat and they were all there on football weekends – home or away.

Writers like Bill Conlin of the Philadelphia Daily News, Frank Bilovsky of the Philadelphia Bulletin, Sandy Padwe of the Philadelphia Inquirer, and later Bill Lyon. One of my favorites was the Pittsburgh Press' Bill Heufelder, a tall, bald, cigar-chomping man who was always smiling, at least on the outside. When I started at the Press in the summer of 1974, Bill even directed me to a furniture guy who gave me a cheap deal on a couch, an end table and a bed for my first apartment, on Ohio River Blvd, west of the city. Plus, he mentored me regarding how things were in the big city for a kid from Palmyra, Pa., population barely 10,000.

When I was a student, working for the Collegian, on home Saturdays I would get player and coach quotes for the Philly and Pittsburgh guys because their deadlines were too tight for them to visit the post-game locker room, which at that time was down the road at the Ice Pavilion, not in the stadium. Grabbing a wad of those old 5-copy carbon sheets, I'd knock out a few graphs of quotes for each of them and pass them out at their desks. I'd usually get 10 bucks from each writer. That was big money for a college kid back then.

Solid friendships that lasted decades into my professional career were made with many of these writers. I remember being at the 1972 Sugar Bowl game between Penn State and Oklahoma, which was then held on New Year's Eve. That morning, Frank Bilovsky knocked on my door at the Fairmont Hotel in New Orleans and was the first to tell me that Roberto Clemente had died in a plane crash, on a mercy mission to his native Nicaragua.

Padwe was responsible for my getting the job in Pittsburgh. He told me right off it was a desk job – an overnight desk job, no less, working 11 p.m. to 7 a.m. – but that I would have the opportunity to "write myself off of the desk." Which I eventually did, grabbing every opportunity for a byline, sometimes working 16-hour days, but it all paid off two years later, when I landed the Steeler beat.

The year before, I was mostly off the desk and writing, sharing the Steeler beat with the amazingly talented Phil Musick, but when Phil jumped to the Post-Gazette in 1976 to be sports editor and columnist, the best sports beat on the paper suddenly was open. After winning what was fondly referred to as "The Great Steeler Writeoff," which our Executive Sports Editor, Don Dillman, conducted so as not to be charged with merely handing me the job, I started the 1976 season as the youngest NFL beat guy in the country at 25.

***

Around town and throughout Central Pennsylvania, the Mirror's presence clearly was larger than either our circulation or our tenure, mostly because of the writing quality of our people and color graphics that back then were fairly uncommon.

Our travel budget, however, was as tiny as our ad revenue. We had to really watch expenses and usually drove to the away football games, as long as the trip could be made in 4-6 hours. We often were able to ride the Penn State charters with the team for the long road trips, but I was never comfortable in that surrounding. As I often said, I never wanted to be stuck somewhere where I couldn't leave the room.

Terry drove sometimes, but on one trip to Maryland, in his old Pontiac, we got so drunk after the game that it necessitated an unplanned overnight trip at John Morris' brother's house and a return that next morning.

Then again, my 1965 British Ford wasn't the most reliable car, either. I once dropped two mufflers on a trip to Syracuse.

Another trip, to Morgantown for a WVU game, also stands out. Not because of that bandbox Mountaineer Field – where your feet were on the Astroturf if you sat in the front row – but more so the overall culture.

The bar was called The Castle, as I recall, and we stayed there for quite a while, mesmerized by dozens of WVU girls, who were built more like wrestlers, chugging that nasty 3.2 beer from Stroh's quart bottles.

Talk about different times. I was covering the 1974 Orange Bowl game between Penn State and LSU for the Mirror. Sitting next to Bill Lyon of the Philadelphia Inquirer, I remember telling him about the added pressure I was under. Miss our late deadline with the game story and it will cost the paper a whole 200 bucks in overtime.

I made the deadline, as I always did, and the Mirror had an extra $200 to spend. But heck, that almost covered two week's pay for me.

I never did find out whether I received praise or indifference from Paul Houck, the Mirror's Executive Editor, for my Orange Bowl performance. After all, his communication skills, for somebody in the communications business, could be a bit unorthodox.

When you walked into Houck's office and asked him a question, sometimes instead of answering verbally, he would swivel over to his typewriter, peck out his answer on a pink memo slip, and hand it to you, with no accompanying words.

Strange, a bit like everything else at the Mirror, but I always will be grateful that Paul allowed Terry to hire me.

John (Beaver) Andrews was the stabilizing force in the Mirror sports department. A little older, and a lot more mature. Our opinions or styles were seldom edited away, but Beaver (or his wife Jane) were there to let you know if you overstepped your journalistic freedom at any point. After all, with our teetering financial situation, Lord knows we couldn't survive even a small lawsuit.

Terry was, without a doubt, the perpetual writing machine. The stories just kept coming and coming. He just kept typing. Not hurriedly, but smoothly and steadily. A paper with this much space was made for Terry. He would have gone crazy at USA Today, writing 10-inch, hold-to-the-front blurbs. At the Mirror it was nothing for him to write three or four stories every night, sometimes more, plus headlines and photo cutlines, and then help Beaver with laying out the paper.

If the Associated Press Sports Editors gave out awards for volume, Terry would have won it every year.

The genius of the department, of course, was Dennis Gildea, whose T. Wes Brillik character was so weirdly wonderful and totally unique. Underneath that green eyeshade, Dennis seemed a throwback to an earlier time in newspapers and just being around him was special, hearing a daily medley of his colorful phrases in that coal country PA accent.

To me, it always felt like Dennis was just passing through our little station in time, and we were all better for it, as journalists and as human beings.

I regret not having kept in touch with Dennis after I left State College. He was always so much deeper than what was happening around us, with that little, smirky grin suggesting he knew something that we did not.

As much as we knew beating the CDT was futile considering its history and how solidly its advertisers were positioned, it was fun to fight the fight, my brief stay notwithstanding. I was proud to have a small part in the experience. We liked the CDT guys, and it was never a hostile situation.

I remember Ron Bracken of the CDT and I covering a State College High-Pittsburgh Central Catholic game in the fall of 1973. We kept our own stats back in those days, on a notepad, walking the sidelines. Not my forte, by any means, and the next day in the paper, I noticed that my stats in the Mirror were about 150 yards different than his in the CDT.

When I saw Ron next, I told him, "Ron, we don't have to be right. We just have to agree. Nobody is going to know but you and me."

I'd like to think that the CDT guys read our stories every day, laughed at how loosely we were able to write and got just a little jealous. But, then again, we knew they would be around far longer than us.

As much as I needed to take the Pittsburgh Press job if I was going to realize the big-city dreams I had then, I easily could have stayed another year or so at the Mirror. It was that much fun. It was that satisfying. It was that unique.

I have to say that during no other job in my career did I play soccer or golf in the newsroom.

Nowhere else did I toss beer cans onto the roof.

Nowhere else was I told, write as long as you need to because we have to fill the space.

Nowhere else did I sit around the desk with my colleagues, scanning an early run of the paper past midnight, finally sipping a beer with the deadline officially passed, and feel more proud.

Nowhere else but the Mirror.

CHAPTER 12
DON'T GET MARRIED AND LEAVE!

By Denise Bowman-Scott

Paul Houck gazed over his brown-frame glasses.

"How do I know that, if I hire you, you won't go get married and leave?"

ME: (gulp) "Um, you don't, sir."

Thus became the crux of my walk-in interview for a reporter's job with the Pennsylvania Mirror. I was a newly-minted Penn State J-School grad, hoping to leave the charitable temporary nest of the Dutch Pantry restaurant for a REAL job in my field.

DEDICATED –
Denise Bowman-Scott spent five years as a Pa. Mirror reporter.

Over the last 50 years, I have had thoughts of what I shoulda-woulda-mighta said to answer Paul Houck's question, more elaborately, with the Political Correctness of the early 1970s. But I didn't. Because I wanted that job. And I was 21. And my bank account needed more than the stipend pittance from the Penn State Daily Collegian that had kept me afloat for the previous four years.

Hired, I got.

What follows is not in chronological order. But the anecdotes and observations are as close to true as I recall after 50 years. My naiveté about newspaper finances and corporate, competitive finagling and industry changes back then makes me blush today. But I was 21 in a job that I loved (quite blindly, I later determined).

The newsroom I walked into was populated by a clot of characters and miscreants with whom I shared adventures with over the next five years – including competing scribes at the PM Centre Daily Times. Preceding me on my team were **R. Thomas Berner,** managing news editor; **Gerry Lynn Hamilton,** Tom's right hand; **James Woodcock**, the county reporter who plied the courthouse and the state legislature in big-boy clothes; **Kathleen Ewing**, whose job had something to do with Clearfield (the county to the north). And then **Sheila R. Irvine.** She was a mother hen to our staff, my post-deadline drinking buddy at the My-O-My, a wicked pinochle player, bridesmaid at my wedding, a trusted colleague and friend for the rest of her life.

We all had titles and beat assignments. I was the paper's "education reporter." But, in truth, our ranks were always so small that, if anything ever breathed of news and you were available, you were NEXT UP!

On Tuesday, Oct. 19, 1971, John June Tressler Jr. a well-known local Bellefonte junkyard dealer, pulled up his truck, got out his rifle and shot two Bellefonte borough police officers on the main street climbing to the Centre County courthouse during rush hour. Ptl. Ronald D. Seymore, 29, was killed; officer Clarence Seward was injured but survived.

Everybody in the Mirror newsroom was NEXT UP! Some drove to the shooting scene or the Bellefonte Borough police station or the state police barracks or Centre Community Hospital. I was in Sheila Irvine's car. We spent half of forever chasing this story all over Central Pennsylvania and dictating bits and pieces of news developments over the telephone, often with coins involved. (It was a time when the most sophisticated technology available to us on the road were a CB radio, which I had in my car but Sheila did not, and a police scanner.

She had to clean about a 40-gallon-size mountain of fast food wrappers, junk mail, old newspapers' etc. off the front passenger side of her Dodge Dart to make room for me. Turns out Sheila was fastidious about maintaining her car, under the hood and outside. But she also had an expensive, concert-hall quality sound system installed.

The detritus, she told me, was a camouflage to hide the sound system from would-be thieves when she had to park in sketchy areas. Sheila's theory was the dump on the passenger side would shoo bad guys away.

It worked.

***

I look back on our morning-after news product – for which the Mirror later won a heralded and deserved statewide award – and realize how many NEXT UPs, especially from photo, made that issue happen.

John Tressler stood trial – twice! – for this broad-daylight murder. I was not assigned to the first trial, but soaked up courtroom carnival anecdotes from reporters and competitors on the case. Didn't sound like any Perry Mason I had ever seen.

Jaw droppingly, the jury hung.

I was tapped for Round 2 of the Tressler trial, whose defense was every bit as bizarre as before. There wasn't a red herring on the planet that didn't get pulled out during those exhausting days. The Centre Daily assigned **Robert H. Emmers** to this phase. Local broadcast newsies flitted in and out of the courtroom to file hourly updates.

About this time, Tom Berner left for the CDT and the chance to provide financial stability to his wife and young daughter. Replacing him was **David G. Fay**, an impish Irish explosion with astonishing red hair and beard, a mercurial temperament that allowed him to get away with calling in drunk to avoid afternoon meetings with the higher ups and a huge heart. He was a helluva newsman.

Anecdote No. 1

A personal NEXT UP: On my way from Boalsburg village to my regular Sunday Mirror shift when 9 gazillion emergency vehicle lights and sirens roared past me and up the Boalsburg Pike. Sorry, I snoop. I followed and came upon a small plane crash scene (one-half mile away from my eventual in-laws' house. But I digress.}

My job came with a 35mm SLR camera as backup to the photo professionals. I did have two hands-on photojournalism classes at PSU for which my parents paid money. To this day, I can develop 35mm film in a darkroom. And print.

I came upon the crash site. Luckily for me, emergency people kept me far enough back that I could not see the carnage. The 35 mm lens got me closer than I ever want to be again to capture a print-worthy shot of a scene like that and go to work without vomiting. Hours later, Mirror publisher Blair Bice called to ask about the crash. I had to tell him that the dead were friends from his church.

Anecdote No. 2

I was working my Sunday shift in an all-but-deserted building, taking obit information over my headset, my back to the hallway. A polite man over my shoulder said, "Excuse me, ma'am." I rang off the funeral home and swiveled to see the man.

There, a foot from my face, was the head and shoulders of a dead buck deer that was draped over the man's arm. The face of the deer stared blankly into mine.

It seemed the hunter had bagged a big one the day before and wanted the Mirror to take a picture for the paper. We had never done that but I scrambled to the photo office and begged the part-timer on duty to take a photo. Higher-ups could decide what to do with it later. The photo was taken and the hunter received a print, which sent him off happy. I never heard from the hunter again.

This doesn't happen in the 'burbs.

***

I was among some news-side colleagues who had viewed newspaper photographers as "decorators" to our REAL JOURNALISM. We tolerated the grip-and-grinners, check-passers and staged bullshit. And spent zero time covering sports, which was bad on us.

And then came **Don Black**. Our assignment was to interview a couple who has been held hostage by escapees from Rockview, the state prison nearby, and lived to tell us. It was not my finest hour as a reporter. I walked in, "winging it" with moron questions: "How did you feel…" Shudder, shudder.

But Don Black engaged these sweet, traumatized people. Asking about framed photos in their living room. How long they had lived in the house (where they had just been held hostage). Kids grow up there? Engaging in neighborly chatter: "I never thought of locking the door between the garage and the kitchen; now I will."

In that moment, on a minor story, the thunderbolt hit me: there are PHOTOJOURNALISTS in this world and I had just worked with a superb one. He made the couple forget the camera draped over his neck.

I got more for my story from Don's easy conversation than my own inept questions. They loved Don. I did too.

The Sunday Paper

My first thought about this section was to subtitle it, with much snark: "snatching defeat from the jaws of victory." Consider: The Mirror launched a Sunday paper with exclusive local coverage of a national NCAA powerhouse football team and the explosive growth of college sports. Our CDT competition published Saturday afternoons with lots of local prep-school results from Friday night – and then not again until Monday afternoon.

This left this massive 36-hour news hole into which the Mirror could shovel a boatload of local content — - color photos, crafted features, an occasional blockbuster, plenty of police, fire and breaking news — -before CDT people ever needed to roll out of bed again.

The Saturday sports coverage, even after Penn State football season, was still manna from heaven from a news perspective. We had 1.5 days as a local print paper to offer up, unanswered, the best content we could muster. Heady times. Sounded, to my newsie head, like a fantastic opportunity to kick the Old Grey Lady's butt, shore up finances, rocket-launch home delivery subscriptions.

Should have happened. Didn't. And I don't know why.

In later years, at many other newspapers, I got hints. (Cutthroat ad competition, skullduggery, developing Big Money sports, the Old Boy network) But at The Mirror, young newsies like me had one job: deliver superior, original, news content. So, we got on our hamster wheel and picked off the best of the low-hanging fruit in a county rich with untapped real news. It wasn't that the CDT was lazy. I enjoyed competing with many of them. Beat and got beaten a time or two. It just seemed that the Centre Daily viewed the Mirror as a swarm of annoying fruit flies that could be swatted away at any time when they got around to it.

Celebrities

Penn State, a major university sprung up in the nowheresville of rural Pennsylvania, often attracted speakers-bureau bookings from celebrities touting a new book, releasing a new album, keeping their profiles public between big-city paying gigs. I hated them! Many of us would scramble to avoid drawing the short straw that would end with an evening with the likes of Ravi Shankar or Joan Baez and the inevitable post speech news conference. But it was a "we were there" imperative and we largely sucked it up and did it. There were entertaining speakers – Rod Serling blew me away, for example, as did the Rev. Ralph Abernathy. One of the Mirror's newer reporters, music aficionado **Robert Trump** (now deceased)**,** was obsessed with folk rocker Don McLean of "American Pie" fame and called in all his chips to get assigned to McLean's performance.

This leads me to the Great Dan Rather Kerfluffle. The CDT's Terry Dalton and I were assigned to this Watergate-era speech. Other than Walter Cronkite, Dan Rather was among the more high-profile newsmen in broadcasting during that heady time. Terry and I filed our stories and went out for coffee with Rather at The Corner Room restaurant in the State College Hotel. By the next day, it was clear our stories diverged about whether or not Rather said he thought Richard Nixon would resign in the coming months. A stink was made in the local news-watching community. One of us evidently had dropped the ball and our credibility was on the line.

I also "knew a guy" in radio who had recorded the whole speech on tape. I got a copy, cued up support for my version, in Rather's unmistakable voice, and played it for Paul Houck, Blair Bice and anyone else who would listen. Paul penned an editorial excerpting the quote that supported my version and I was feeling exonerated.

But, in fairness, a later review of the whole tape provided ample evidence that supported Terry's (opposite) take on that speech. My first lesson as a newbie newsie that day was that sometimes important people talk out of both sides of their mouths. Served me well to remember that in later years.

We were never briefed on the financial/operational state of the company. If anyone else had been besides Paul Houck and Blair Bice, it might have been Dave Fay. But, if so, he kept his counsel. And we toddled along on our hamster wheels trying to crank out the best stuff we could find with the ominous financial whispers all around us.

Change was inevitable.

Trump replaced Woodcock. Later, six of his Sigma Chi fraternity brothers perished in a fiery crash in Maryland. I handled the Mirror's news story and the obituary information. I knew one of the Sigma Chis well and attended his funeral.

Perri Foster-Pegg did features, filled in for the family page editor and cranked through her share of government meetings. **Jean**

Reeve came along on the copy desk until she and her husband, the Daily Collegian's publisher, decamped for Easton, PA. Cathy Ewing succumbed to Type 1 diabetes.

After the Tressler trial and the ensuing Hurricane Agnes flooding, Emmers and I dated, then married and spent the next two years concerned about our family's financial eggs in the same basket. Emmers was disappointed at the official reaction to his well-sourced expose about fire safety in a well-known State College landmark and his inability to persuade Paul and Blair to green-light its publication. "It was the best-read story never published" a Penn State J-school professor often quipped. But I know the whole matter hurt. When an opportunity came for Emmers to edit a small afternoon paper in upstate New York, he seized it. There was something in it for me too: the chance to establish and run a bureau for the southern third of Chenango County.

We were there for about 18 months; Billings, Mt. for another 18, and Tidewater, Va. after that. We were good about the marriage vows thing until about the seventh year, when Emmers stumbled. After our split, I returned to journalism in Tidewater for nearly a decade. It was there, in Virginia Beach, that I met and married Robert J. Scott. We had two daughters in the late 80s and I morphed into a full-time volunteer PTA mom, which I loved. We lost Bob, Aug. 1, 2018, after 38 years of marriage, to cancer spawned by his exposure to Agent Orange in Vietnam.

Paul Houck was right that, if he hired me back in 1971, I might go get married and leave him and the Mirror. It did, however, take me five years. I think he got a pretty good bargain.

CHAPTER 13
HOW THE MIRROR SAVED MY LIFE

By Perri (Foster-Pegg) Capell

My stint at the Pennsylvania Mirror lasted eight months, but it helped save my life. In 1972, four months after I graduated from Penn State, the paper hired me on as a staff reporter. It was a lucky break. Not everyone could get a newspaper reporter's job in those days, due to a generally weak economy in the '70s.

I had little experience plus, unbeknownst to everyone — even me — I was recovering from a mental health crisis. It had caused me to lose my first job after college at The Warren Times Observer in my home town of Warren, Pa. Fortunately, it so happened that the Mirror's city editor, Dave Fay, had also worked for the Warren Times Observer in the early 1960s. Fay, never much known for sentimentality, apparently took an interest in me because of this connection.

So the Mirror job was a second chance. Besides being able to return to daily newspapering, I looked forward to leaving Warren, where I was living with my parents, and

SURVIVOR – Perri Foster-Pegg Capell regained her focus at the Mirror before moving on to a productive career in newspapers. (Photo courtesy of Perry Capell)

returning to State College, Pa., the Mirror's home base and where I had a lively time at PSU.

The Mirror was forced to close a few years after I left, unfortunately. I didn't do much to save it, but the Mirror saved me, as I'll explain later on. It truly was a grand place to work, full of talented and idiosyncratic people. Besides the remarkable fact that the Mirror opened its doors when other newspapers were closing theirs, the paper became known for hiring gifted young journalists and allowing them to write inventive stories.

To some degree, I might have fit that ticket, because after the Mirror, I went on to have a varied and successful career, with journalism and writing as its central theme. The last full-time job I held was a 15-year stint at The Wall Street Journal and other Dow Jones & Co. publications.

At any rate, green as I was, Mirror executive editor Paul Houck and city editor Dave Fay saw something and gave me a secure place to learn, polishing my stories and putting up with my antics.

Fay assigned articles and let us hunt down our own. At 21, I was immature; basically, I didn't know what I didn't know. The Mirror's senior reporters generously gave me much-needed writing tips. I will be forever grateful to reporter Denise Bowman for changing my passive writing approach. Use "is" not "was" in your leads, she told me. "Don't back into your sentences." Robert Emmers, another experienced reporter, let me get away with copying his unique writing style a few times. It didn't seem so at the time, but Fay, who could impale me with one look from his piercing Irish eyes, was actually kind and patient with me.

Starting My Journo Career

The job was a big rung on my career ladder. I became passionate about journalism after joining The Daily Collegian at Penn State. I discovered I loved news writing and seeing my name in print. Besides Collegian articles, I wrote a free-lance feature for the Warren newspaper about a PSU student from a well-known Warren family.

I got $15 for the feature and a reporter job for the summer. I typed obituaries, called police departments, and took dictation from "stringers" who covered events in towns close to Warren. My specialty was features about local things: say, the new glass recycling plant or a model airplane club. I was pushy and determined. My best work was a three-part series about the trials Warren women faced if they wanted an illegal abortion (Roe v Wade wasn't law yet). People yelled at or hung up on me when I called them. Ultimately the publisher killed the story, telling me it was too controversial.

Returning to Penn State for my senior year, I felt like a seasoned journalist. The Collegian promoted me to senior news reporter. Sometimes, I wrote features. A personal account for the Collegian sports page about being the first female reporter to enter PSU's Beaver Stadium press box is still floating around the Internet somewhere.

A Little Setback

I left the Collegian and State College in 1972 to spend my final semester studying journalism in England. That prior winter semester, before I flew overseas, I started having difficulty organizing my thoughts and finishing papers. Being an overachiever, I didn't put much stock in it. But after joining other Penn Staters in the mass communications program at Manchester University, my condition worsened.

Mental illness manifests itself differently in everyone. I couldn't stop the constant critical inner dialogue going on in my brain that kept me from enjoying things or making decisions. Going to England to study was a dream come true for me, and I blamed myself for spoiling the opportunity. I cried most days, but didn't know I was struggling with full-blown depression. Still, I somehow finished the program, graduated with honors from PSU and returned to Warren and a promised job at the daily newspaper.

My mental issues didn't stop, however. I had trouble writing and talking coherently. And because I couldn't link my racing thoughts with my speech, I began to stutter. This condition would have been hard for anyone, but it was agonizing for a college graduate who had shown promise as a journalist. I wanted to stick my head in a gas oven, a la Sylvia Plath. Ultimately, I made so many blunders at work that I was fired.

The United Way campaign in Warren needed an assistant to do mundane work, so I jumped at this port in the storm. The mindless activity plus sessions with a mental health counselor helped to end the constant negative self-talk in my brain, stop stuttering and think rationally again. In the midst of this, I got a tip about the Mirror opening, thanks to my Collegian buddy Terry Nau, who had become sports editor of the Mirror.

In late September 1972, I interviewed with Paul Houck, who hired me for about $100 a week. Within a few days, I had an auto loan and a lightly used Chevy Vega. I drove it to State College, and rented a share in an apartment on Beaver Avenue. I was again a working reporter, earning just enough money to live on. It amazes me now: In the midst of recovering from a nervous breakdown, I landed this remarkable job.

Life at the Mirror

It was what I needed. Each day I banged away at a gray manual typewriter, producing stories within deadlines, smoking incessantly (our section of the newsroom was a purple haze, with all but one member of it being a heavy smoker). Our most advanced piece of equipment was an earphone head-set that plugged into our telephones, so we didn't have to grip the phone receiver between neck and shoulder while taking notes. Being in the newsroom, interviewing people, writing articles and seeing my byline in the paper helped me feel like my old self again.

I wrote about meat boycotts, the energy crisis, gas shortages, local opinion surveys, civic club honorees, and why the Centre County United Way didn't meet its financial goal. I did a nice feature about fourth-graders touring a new sewage treatment plant and learning what happened to their poop and pee.

I covered syndicated columnist Jack Anderson's visit to Penn State and Roe v. Wade campaigners in Pennsylvania. And I was the substitute editor of the Mirror's "family page" (formerly the women's page) when the regular editor was out of the office.

My Achilles' heel was local government meetings, e.g. municipal authorities, commissions, etc. I struggled to get facts straight about local taxation, Home Rule, planning and zoning and so forth. When these meetings ended around 9 or 9:30 p.m., I'd speed back to the newsroom and try to submit a semi-coherent story before the 11 p.m. deadline.

Wild-eyed Fay would breathe fire down our necks, loudly reminding us to get our articles done. I'd run to my desk, flip through my notes, light cigarette after cigarette, and type like my life depended on it. Somehow we finished our stories, the copy editor reviewed them and the paper got "put to bed" in time. Dave had us write headlines for our articles (using the now outdated letter-unit-counting system). Then we'd wait for Dave to send the pages to the print department and dismiss us for the night.

Drawbacks

Much as I thought I'd adjust to the paper's 3 p.m. to 11 p.m. (and sometimes later) shift, I really didn't. There wasn't much to do after work except go to the bars and drink with co-workers. We typically convened in the back room of the My-O-My, a State College strip joint/gay bar. I would get home around 3 a.m., then sleep until 11 a.m. There was barely enough time to shower, dress and maybe run an errand before work started again.

Sexism also prevailed at the Mirror, though I didn't know what it was back then because like so many women, I was so used to it. But as in many workplaces, some heavy-duty testosterone floated around the Mirror, particularly in the sports section.

The way the news room was arranged, reporters like me had to walk by the sports department to get to our desks. Each day, I had to walk past two of three sports reporters, who often made snarky remarks. I didn't know how to defend myself. These guys did it because they could, but it wasn't really about me. Men in general were allowed to ridicule women at work.

I have no clue what other reporters thought about my abilities. But as much as I tried to write well, I felt they were better. I was sort of the fluff writer. Meanwhile, Denise didn't take shit from anyone and wrote hard-hitting front-page stories. So did Robert Emmers. There was another strong reporter named Sheila Irvine, while Jean Reeve was our copy editor (plus the only one of us who was happily married). Fay ruled over this motley group with an iron fist.

I don't remember having a personal conversation with Dave other than to get details about assignments and a few remarks about working in Warren. He was a no-nonsense newspaper man, loved professional sports and scared the bejesus out of me. That's probably why I didn't get to know him better.

Living above the Brewery

Romance wasn't as easy for me as a working girl in State College as it was when I was a student. If you finish work at 11 p.m., going to the bars is the only *choix de la nuit*. Plus I only had to step out my front door on Beaver Avenue, and I was practically inside The Brewery. No kidding, my apartment was on top of this renowned dive bar. Sure, the Brewery was convenient and living above it seemed Hemingway-esque, but I didn't make enough money to be buying many bar drinks. And when its drunk clientele left in the wee hours, the yelling and shattering glass diminished the allure.

Still, a social life – however paltry — was a priority for me. I was always starting or ending short relationships. Most eligible prospects socialized late at night like me. Once I hooked up with a musician in a local rock band. The band's biggest problem was not having a truck to move their equipment. Because I worked for the Mirror, I had access to its fleet of vans. At least once I took a Mirror van to move the band's stuff; it's possible that's why the musician liked me (briefly).

Of course, being immature and headstrong, I didn't ask for permission to use the van for the band. Then, in an unmitigated bit of chutzpah, I infuriated Dave and was nearly fired for doing the same thing again, not asking him if I could take a Mirror vehicle for personal use. It turned out that my '71 Chevy Vega, bought for $1,200 at an auto auction, was a lemon. The car had electrical problems (very costly), guzzled oil and spewed smoke, and we suspected the odometer had been turned back.

Little did I know that those problems were endemic to the Vega. (The Vega is *"an unmitigated disaster,"* Automotive News intoned.) I hated the car and my monthly car loan payments, so I poured copious amounts of oil and STP into the engine and sold it through the classifieds.

As soon as the car was gone, I was desperate to pay off the loan. The Warren bank that lent me the money told me I had to close it in person. I charged into the Mirror newsroom and found Dave. In verbatim, I said, *"I'm asking you — no, I am telling you — that I'm taking a company vehicle to Warren."* I roll my eyes just thinking about it. From State College, it's a five-hour round trip through the Allegheny Forest to Warren and back. This memory is seared in my brain because Fay was so pissed, he wouldn't look at or talk to me for a week.

Being headstrong, and lacking a personal car, I became creative about getting to work. Sometimes staffers gave me rides, but if not, I hitch-hiked three miles up the Benner Pike, a remarkably dangerous thing to do. It's amazing I survived my own stupidity.

Opportunity Knocks

The winter of 72-73 was cold and snowy and seemed endless. State College can get amazingly slushy, plus I hadn't known how eerily deserted the town got when the students went home for semester breaks. Finally, spring came, allowing me to put my snow boots away. In May 1973, I celebrated my 22nd birthday in the bars. I had been at the Mirror for about 8 months and now drove a 1967 VW bug. My depression had lifted, I wrote somewhat proficiently, the sports guys didn't bother me much anymore, and I had no plans to leave.

But out of the blue, I got a job offer from that P.R. agency I had worked for in Warren. It did the publicity for Chautauqua Institution, a historic gated performing-arts community on the shores of Chautauqua Lake, N.Y. During college, I had waitressed at hotels within its gates and had come to love the place.

The job as summer publicity director meant running the Chautauqua press office for three months that year. I wanted it, so I asked Dave for a leave of absence, pledging to return to the Mirror in September. He gave me his blessing, and I headed off to Chautauqua. "She'll never return," Fay told a friend.

He was right. I never did.

Since then…

In short, the months I spent at the Mirror helped save my life. I had healed from near mental paralysis and learned to produce good copy. In my subsequent career, I've used many reporting and writing skills I learned at the Mirror. I was a reporter and editor for The Trenton Times when it was owned by The Washington Post; I had the same roles later at Dow Jones & Co. Inc. for 15 years.

In 1998, my first husband died and I became a single mother, living in New Jersey. The population and traffic congestion were so overwhelming that I packed the kids and our Rottweiler in an SUV and drove to Boise, Idaho, where I continued to work remotely for the WSJ. On the emptier Idaho roads, I learned to ride a motorcycle. Motorcycle magazines need good feature writers, and once I could "keep the shiny side up," I pitched them ideas. My motorcycle feature assignments took me on expense-paid trips around the world: Oman, New Zealand, Norway, Vietnam, Laos, Canada and throughout the U.S.

I still work part-time, mostly doing things I like. For my next act, who knows? Maybe I'll pick up motorcycle riding again.

CHAPTER 14
GONE BUT NOT FORGOTTEN

By Bill Horlacher

(EDITOR'S NOTE: This material has been updated from a December 2017 column that originally appeared in statecollege.com.)

Maybe it's understandable that most residents of Centre County remember little or nothing of an upstart newspaper from their region. After all, the Pennsylvania Mirror was laid to rest when its final edition appeared on Dec. 31, 1977. The Mirror is dead, buried and all but forgotten.

BILL HORLACHER
... *fond memories*

But on the other hand, how could such a free-wheeling publication ever be lost from memory? Yes, 40-plus years is a long time, but surely there's room in the county's lore for some tales of this groundbreaking newspaper.

From its birth on Dec. 11, 1968 as the step child of the Altoona Mirror, the new publication introduced dramatic changes to local journalism. Printed on a state-of-the-art offset press, the Mirror showcased color photography and other innovations. And it also demonstrated the viability of morning circulation. The Mirror arrived in the wee hours of the morning — most of the time, at least. Back then, the Centre Daily Times was an evening paper, and it did not wake up to smell the coffee until 1986.

Youthful & Aggressive

Readers soon picked up another difference — a youthful, aggressive approach in the writing. "The Mirror was a child of the '60s," said Chris Koll, a sportswriter for the publication. "It was flippant, it was irreverent."

The initial staff of the Mirror felt a certain cockiness about the future. "We were gung-ho," recalled Tom Berner, the paper's assistant sports editor, who later became its city editor. "I think we thought we were going to be better than the CDT."

Before long, however, reality struck and Mirror writers realized that the well established Centre Daily Times held sway in State College and surrounding areas. "I think we had the feeling that we were certainly the second place, lesser light newspaper in town," said Dennis Gildea, a former sportswriter and columnist with the *Mirror*. "I think that was particularly true in sports where a lot of the things we did were meant to be good journalism, but they were also meant to stick it to the CDT or the administration at Penn State."

"The CDT was much more buttoned down," said Koll, a former Penn State wrestler whose father, Bill Koll, was the Nittany Lions' grappling coach in the late '60s and the '70s. "As far as doing what a newspaper is supposed to do, maybe the CDT was actually fulfilling its role better than the Mirror. But if you wanted to be entertained, there wasn't any comparison. When you wrote for the Mirror, you didn't just want to write a story, you wanted to write a story that was fun to read."

Cuttig Loose after Deadlines

And the emphasis on fun didn't end when a writer submitted a story. A morning paper demanded evening work by its reporters, and sportswriters stayed especially late to write stories after nighttime contests. Gildea, Koll and other colleagues often found ways to cut loose after meeting their deadlines around 11:30 p.m.

"You'd cover a high school football game or some kind of event, and you'd slam the story out," said Koll, now a high school wrestling coach and executive with a Syracuse-area construction company. "Then people would always bring in beers. So everyone would be sitting back with their feet up, drinking beer. And then Gildea would bring in some sort of athletic equipment (Wiffle ball or Nerf football). So then as you were drinking beers, you'd be having these athletic contests over the top of the news desk."

Perhaps more than any other Mirror scribe, Gildea personified the satirical personality of the publication. Not only did he spearhead office athletics, but he served as the anonymous author of the paper's wackiest feature — a weekly column of sports prognostications by the fictitious character known as T. Wes Brillik.

Who was T. Wes Brillik?

In Gildea's vivid imagination, Brillik lived with his wife, Mimsy, on Mount Nittany and enjoyed downing Utica Clubs ("UCs") at Bellefonte's now-defunct Big Trout Inn. Brillik spoke in a unique dialect where the Mirror became "the Mirrow," wrestlers were "rasslers" and Penn State was "Nit U." Occasionally, Brillik's full name (Thaddeus Westmoreland Brillik) was shared with readers, but prior to a 2017 column in statecollege.com, no public admission of Gildea's authorship was ever published.

The goal of Brillik's utterances, said Gildea, was "striking a consistent tone with Joe Paterno who didn't want football to be the most important thing in anyone's life." So, because he felt that Penn

State players and State College High School players should avoid taking themselves too seriously, Gildea's Brillik almost always predicted victories by the opposition.

"I remember one time," said Gildea, "I think they were playing Temple, and I did pick Penn State to win — I mean, Brillik did. But the score was going to be 2-0." As for State High predictions, Brillik must have needed to rassle with his conscience to favor Little Lion opponents during the early 1970s. Somehow, despite State High's 36-game winning streak, Gildea persisted in picking their foes.

Gildea died in May of 2020, but those who wish to plumb Mirror archives will still be delighted by his Brillik offerings. As often as not, Gildea/Brillik would include a bit of unedited poetry to make a point — like this warning he gave football fans one September that their hearts might soon be broken.

> 'Tis a hard, hard road we have to hoe
> with many a fray before the snow
> of winter comes to blanket the turf
> With its white mantle so purf,
> just like the slates of football teams
> starting out now with unbeaten dreams
> till along comes Thanksgiving and ol' Tom Turkey
> & all those gridiron realities so murkey.
> So gimme a sis, a boom and a bah
> Cheer so loud your throats turns rah
> let it all hang out like ol' reckless boozers
> cause chances are your team'll be feckless loosers."

Serious News Coverage

Apart from their light-hearted pursuits, Mirror people also produced award-winning news stories and in-depth features. The staff compiled a 48-page tabloid to chronicle the devastating floods from Hurricane Agnes in 1972, and some 100,000 copies were sold across Pennsylvania. Another special publication that celebrated the

September 1970 opening of the "Keystone Shortway" (the original name for Pennsylvania's piece of Interstate 80) drew widespread appreciation. And a team of Mirror reporters, in 1971, delivered highly-professional coverage of the murder of a Bellefonte policeman, Ronald D. Seymore, and the manhunt by nearly 200 policemen that succeeded in capturing his killer, John June Tressler.

Perhaps the most memorable news coverage during the Mirror's nine-year history pertained to Apollo 11. Not only was Neil Armstrong's step onto the moon a "giant leap for mankind," but it provided the Mirror with a chance to publish some eye-popping color images. Only the front page headline writer overstepped his role that day ("Mankind approaches the universe"), but in the context of thrilling NASA's achievement, he can be forgiven for such an astronomical exaggeration.

Jim Houck, the older son of Executive Editor Paul Houck, was then just 11, but he remembers his father's excitement over the Mirror's lunar landing issue. "He was really proud of that," said the editor's son, now a Penn State Law professor who retired from the Navy with the rank of Vice Admiral. "It was less than a year after the paper had come into existence. He gave it away, he was so proud of it. And I delivered that edition up and down College Avenue, up and down Beaver Avenue."

An Uphill Battle

Although Paul Houck enjoyed other editorial triumphs with the Mirror, everyone knew he was fighting an uphill battle. State College and Bellefonte merchants did not provide sufficient advertising dollars for two daily newspapers, and the Centre Daily Times controlled the lion's share. Meanwhile, the Mirror's owners sought to strengthen their position by reaching out to surrounding communities like Philipsburg, Tyrone and even Altoona.

"Paul never had the wherewithal to really compete," said Don Black, the Mirror's chief photographer during the early 1970s. "Trying to cover Tyrone, Altoona and that area while still trying to be the local newspaper for Bellefonte and State College — it was too much of a split. And you're doing it with a limited staff. We didn't have the horses to do some of the basic, everyday things that build continuity and regularity in a newspaper."

After leaving the Mirror in 1972, Black's newspaper career took him to New York State (he was nominated for a Pulitzer Prize while serving in Binghamton), California, Oregon, Indiana, Idaho and Wyoming. Having served as a photographer, editor and publisher, Black can now imagine Houck's predicament.

"I don't think any of us appreciated what Paul Houck did during the time we were there. He had a very rough job and was trying to do the best he could with very limited resources.

"After I had been at the Mirror for a year, Paul called me into his office. I had started at $95 a week. He said, 'You've been here a year. You're going to get a raise and go to $100 a week. Now, of course there are other options. Would you be interested in becoming the assistant city editor for graphics and photography which would help you on your resume?' And I said, 'Paul, that sounds pretty good. What does that pay?' And he said, 'That would be instead of the $5.'

"He was doing what he had to do. Every dollar he could save, he would put toward doing something else for the paper. What a good man."

A Leader's Legacy

Houck left the Mirror in March 1976, roughly a year and a half before its demise. I suspect that until the day of his death in 2001, he felt disappointment over the Mirror's apparent failure. But I say "apparent" because the State College area's first morning paper did achieve success in one key endeavor —developing young journalists.

Houck set the tone for this developmental process by giving creative freedom to his young writers, and I observed his approach while working part-time in the sports department from 1969-1971.

Houck called me into his office one day to see if I felt confident enough to cover the Bellefonte team at the Pennsylvania Teener League baseball championships in Schuylkill County. I was only 17 years old, and I would be driving a company car, using a company camera and producing stories and photos with no oversight. Houck was the Executive Editor, but his questions seemed more dad-like than boss-like. He wasn't going to micro-manage my work; he just wanted to make sure that I and the company car would both return to the office intact.

As for those who apprenticed at the Mirror and then achieved success in other locations, Black ended his career as publisher of the Laramie Boomerang. Berner was recruited to join the Centre Daily Times as an editor in 1971 and then taught journalism at Penn State from 1975 to 2003. Terry Nau (his name rhymes with "now" but Brillik called him "Nay-you") served as sports editor for the Pawtucket Times. Dave Fay covered hockey for the Washington Times for several decades and won a lifetime achievement award from the Hockey Hall of Fame. Dave Bloss served as sports editor for The Providence Journal and then went on to train journalists in developing nations.

And then there was Dennis Gildea, yes, the one-of-a-kind Dennis Gildea. Lots more educated than his buddy Brillik, Gildea held a PhD in mass communications and served on the faculty at Springfield College after he left central Pennsylvania. Not bad for a guy who felt comfortable with Brillik-style statements like, "I'm learnin' to write good."

The End of the Road

Inevitably, the tragic word came down from the newspaper's Blair County owners. They could no longer sustain the *Mirror's* financial losses, and they would shut it down at the end of 1977.

Berner, for one, was "not surprised," adding that "the writing was on the wall for a long time." As for Gildea, though he had also worked for the Centre Daily Times, he said, "It was genuinely tragic, a shame that it didn't survive. We didn't realize we were as talented as we were. We should have flourished more than we did, but from a professional journalistic approach, we never took ourselves seriously enough."

Dead, buried, forgotten. Of the Mirror's unique voices, only T. Wes Brillik survived as long as 2017 when he produced this final poem. It was accompanied by a Gildea comment noting that his alter ego "is pretty sure that next season the Nit gridders'll lose every game."

A Scribe's Interview with T. Wes Brillik

Squintin his beady eyes at the mist offa the fen,
T. Wes Brillik his own self heard the voice again.
"Thaddy, Thaddy, youns gotta get on the hook,"
Mimsy was howlin, so's that's all it took.
Rapped in his Purple Behemoth rasslin robe,
T. Wes his own self slammed the hook to his lobe.
"Wot the dooce do youns want?" Brillik demanded.
"An interview bout the Mirrow," the lad all but commanded.
"The Mirrow," Brillik mused, "is dead and I'm pretty old,
But I'll tells youns this here, the UCs are still cold,
And for this here tale, that's all's needs be told."

CHAPTER 15
THE WRESTLING SPORTSWRITER

By Chris Koll

(EDITOR'S NOTE: Chris Koll wrestled for Penn State's varsity squad, coached by his father, the legendary Bill Koll, and also did free-lance work for the Pennsylvania Mirror sports department. Chris describes the balancing act in this story.)

For the brief period of time I worked as sportswriter for the Pennsylvania Mirror, I never pretended to be a journalist. I thought of myself more as a college wrestler on my father's Penn State team who was open to any form of creativity, on the mat, in the classroom, and with my sometimes rowdy teammates.

When Mirror sports editor Terry Nau hired me in 1974 as a stringer — kind of an adjunct member of the sports staff who worked on a game-by-game basis — my background in news writing was limited to an elective high school journalism course and contributions to the monthly State College High School newspaper. I suspect that Nau assumed with my status as a local athlete, I

PRINT THE LEGEND –
Chris Koll's creative talent was evident during his brief stint as a "stringer" for the Mirror sports department.

possessed a solid grounding in the fundamentals of various sports and could accurately relate the details of a game, match or race.

But if truth be told — outside of wrestling — I knew precious little about any sport. Well, let me amend that. As a male growing up in Central Pennsylvania, it's impossible not to know the basics of the major sports — but so far as understanding tactics, techniques, strategies or plays — I remained clueless.

And so it was with some trepidation that I showed up for my first assignment. It was a high school football game. I can't remember where — probably at Bellefonte or Bald Eagle or Philipsburg — and as Terry had advised me to do, I stood on the sidelines with my clipboard, right beside the linesmen with their down markers, and kept record of the plays.

A more knowledgeable observer might have noted: Off tackle by number 25 results in nine yards, or dive play by number 22 results in 15 yards with crushing block by 33 — but I had no idea what actual plays were being run beyond registering a run up the middle, run around end or pass.

As the game wound down, a theme would start to emerge. I can't remember what it was that particular evening, but it almost always happened. Maybe an underdog was staging an upset, an unheralded performer recording a breakout performance, a team engineering a comeback after a dismal first half: but there had to be a tale to tell.

And if there was no obvious story, then by God it was up to me to devise one! Maybe the weather could be drawn into the conversation, or the fervor of the crowd or some other foreign factor that would lend special significance to what, in reality, was just another athletic event.

Football season segued into the winter sports season. Then spring and summer. I covered scholastic basketball games, wrestling matches, baseball games. After a year, I advanced to covering selected Penn State sports events. And with experience, I gained a deeper understanding of the sports but never let details get in the way of the story.

Was it always totally factual? Honest? An unbiased gathering of just the facts? No. But writing for the Mirror was seldom dull or boring.

***

Terry didn't realize this when he granted me employment — but there was one aspect of working at the Mirror for which I was uniquely qualified. When on assignment to a Friday night game, I'd rush out of the venue following the final whistle and drive at breakneck speed back to the Mirror offices on the Benner Pike. During the drive I'd also hope for the epiphany where I recognized how to describe the game I had just witnessed.

Depending on the location of the game, I'd arrive at the Mirror around 10 p.m. Deadline was midnight. John Andrews, our layout editor, would tell me how many pages of copy I needed to produce to fill the space he'd allocated in the next day's sports page for my story.

Writing on deadline was as close to performing in an athletic competition as you can get without breaking a sweat. There was tremendous pressure to execute in a limited period of time. A misspelled word or an awkward phrase were like a fumble or passed ball — a disastrous mistake that couldn't be repaired. There just wasn't time!

And, like an athletic competition, the result of your efforts would be on public display. Not just to a gym of spectators — but to thousands of readers perusing your words over their morning coffee.

It was tremendously exhilarating.

Stories were filed by midnight and afterwards the newsroom would resemble a post-game locker room. Often, beers were brought out. A surprisingly short amount of time later, usually by 2 a.m., the first copies of the next day's paper would roll off the press.

We'd evaluate our performance, feet up on desks, beer in hand, studying the still-wet newsprint. Like a coach reviewing game film, you were never sure whether the story resonated — if the night was a win or a loss — until you actually saw it in print.

I guess I was part of what was called "The Grand Experiment." This was the catch phrase coined to promote the illusion that the talents of Nittany Lion athletes extended beyond their chosen sports. That they were dedicated students with a variety of additional skills and abilities. The fact that I had an occasional by-line in the morning paper somehow identified me as special.

Now make no mistake. I know for a fact that Penn State then and now maintained higher academic entrance requirements than many institutions. But it always seemed pretentious that some mysterious experiment involving student athletes was being successfully conducted at PSU — as opposed to how other institutions of higher learning handled their affairs.

Besides, I knew better. Aside from their athletic gifts, Penn State athletes were pretty much like the rest of the student population: we included great scholars, average students and those that just got by with the assistance of an occasional crib sheet. There were devout Christians and hell-raising reprobates. Respecters of authority and those willing to bend the rules.

But back in the 1970s, "The Grand Experiment" was a myth we all ascribed to. More's the pity. Because we all contributed to the perilous perch that Penn State athletics attempted to balance on. One that decades later detractors were more than willing to topple.

***

Perhaps the most talented of the assemblage at the Mirror was Dennis Gildea. Dennis never referred to himself as a reporter or journalist. He preferred the term "scribe."

The definition of scribe is a writer, one who primarily works at a newspaper. I like to believe that Dennis — like me — saw himself primarily as a writer who never let a few details get in the way of yarning a good story.

But for me the process was unsustainable. I simply ran out of stories. Other members of the newsroom could rely upon their journalistic training. They were pros. But once my well ran dry, I had nothing to write and left the Mirror in 1975.

I still think of myself as a scribe. Over the intervening years, I penned articles for a local paper in Ridgway, PA., where I taught and coached for seven years. Served as the volunteer editor for American Whitewater — the journal of a national whitewater boating organization for five years. Wrote promotional releases for a whitewater rafting company here in the Adirondacks of New York, where I have lived for many years, running a construction company and coaching high school wrestlers.

And throughout I've followed the lesson learned while writing for the Mirror. One that can be summarized in the final line of the great movie, The Man Who Shot Liberty Valance:

"When the legend becomes fact, print the legend."

Especially if it makes for a good story.

CHAPTER 16
FEATURE WRITER AND FARMER

By Sara Pitzer

My job at the Pennsylvania Mirror lasted less than two years before the paper stopped publishing. My time there led indirectly to my publishing several cookbooks and, eventually, to my job at the Salisbury Post, in North Carolina, where I started as a features writer, then business reporter. I published a weekly humor column and, when I retired, continued on a freelance basis to write food pages. But this is all hindsight, of course, and I had no idea such positive things were in the offing.

FUNNY LADY – *Sara Pitzer could write, talk and smile with the best of them. (Photo courtesy of Sara Pitzer)*

I went to work at the Mirror because it was the only job I could get, and I knew I was stuck in Centre County for the foreseeable future because my husband, Croy, loved his job at the radio station – WMAJ. I tried first to get a job at the Centre Daily Times but it did not happen, even though Jerry Weinstein, the editor, kept me in his office for almost two hours.

At the Mirror, I was interviewed by Paul Houck,

the executive editor. He was vague about opportunities, suggesting maybe they would like to have a "bicentennial desk" to cover events related to the upcoming bicentennial. I left discouraged since such anniversaries come and go, which meant that would be a temporary position. But about a week later, Houck called me and asked if I'd like to "take a whirl" at being the editor of the woman's page.

I took it. It was a job. But I was not real enthusiastic about something aimed specifically at women. Admittedly, it was still an era when women were perceived as "different" in their interests but this was not an attitude I supported. The pay was a whopping $6,000 a year – low even by standards of 1976.

I don't recall any training except the comment by the outgoing woman's editor that the telephone book was my "friend." To this day I am not sure what that meant. I could have used some instruction on how to lay out a page, something I'd never done before. Before the woman's editor I met, the position may have been filled by Jane Andrews, wife of John Andrews, one of the sportswriters. Lining up interviews and writing features was pretty much second nature, something I'd done for Grit, the weekly published in Williamsport, Pa. for a long time.

In one of my early layout attempts, Houck said he noticed that I'd used two-line headlines – known as "heds" in newspaper lingo. "We don't do that," he said. I asked if there was a book I could consult for instruction but he said, "We don't necessarily go by the book. Look at the sports pages."

I don't recall what I learned that way but I must have gotten it right at some point because Houck never mentioned it again.

I quickly learned newsroom lingo – the lead to a story was written as "lede" and a headline was "hed." The woman's editor was not like any other job at the paper. For one thing, I had an office with glass windows inside and others that opened to the outside of the building. My office was actually next to Houck's near the back of the building. We were "guarded" by Carolyn Weldon, who had a desk near my office. I think she must have been the receptionist.

She was a stern woman, very smart but with an acerbic personality. (I learned that she was brilliant at math and financial investments but such jobs were not available to women at the time, so she was probably bitter, too.)

Some things had to run: Ann Landers, some public information stories from Penn State and any upcoming events. The rest was features that it was up to me to find. I usually took a photographer, Dave Hamilton, with me. One of my first stories had this hed: "Meet a local collector." I don't remember what she collected but I do remember Hamilton setting up a picture of her holding something in a way that was obviously staged.

Hamilton loved photographing scenes that involved fire trucks. One I remember was his picture of a firefighter holding an oxygen mask for a small cat. The problem with this, however sweet, was that sometimes when I needed a photographer, Hamilton was chasing a fire truck. The obvious solution was to get a camera and take my own pictures. Hamilton wanted me to buy a Nikon, like his, but it was expensive and the guy at the photo shop convinced me to try a Cannon FTB. I got that, with three lenses, a 100 mm for distance and closer, a 50 or "normal" and a 35 for wide angle. I used the long lens almost exclusively. I would take the pictures and give the film to Hamilton (I think he had a helper, too) to be developed for the paper. I still have a lot of those negatives in an old shoebox somewhere.

I never got a flash attachment since most of the photos I took were outside, but when I was sent to cover a conference with Gloria Steinem I had a problem because it was indoors. The best I could do was to wait until the television crew used their lights to shoot an interview and take my own pictures quickly. The results were a little odd but usable. The conference was about abortion. I took notes and was on the way to a fairly routine story until at the end of the session I met a young woman in the restroom who said she'd had an abortion and, with tears in her eyes, said she regretted it now. I added that to the end of my story and I thought it was a strong ending.

Unfortunately, this was pre-computer editing days and what they used to do was simply cut off the end that did not fit. My addition did not fit. I still remember that.

Usually what went on my page was more routine – mostly local – except where I could slip in some feminist story. The local community theater, Boal Barn, got a lot of coverage, sometimes with just a photo of a performer and a cutline. I ran a photo like that of a woman in the current play with a brief note underneath. In my layout it was next to the Ann Landers column, which I gave the hed, "The Whole Thing Smells." A few days later I got a note from the husband of the community theater woman whose picture I'd run saying, "Thanks for the best laugh I've had in weeks." It took me all day to figure out that he had associated the "smells" hed with the picture of his wife. At least he was amused.

This was an occasion when city editor Dave Fay should have tossed the page down on my desk and said, "What's wrong with this page?" Actually, he did not ever say, he more or less shouted. Fay had two tones, loud and louder. But he missed this one. Once when he pulled that stunt and I could not answer, he said, "Talk to Andrews," and stalked off. John Andrews, JDA to me, "Beaver" to the other sports guys, said it looked like a good page to him.

The sports crew worked later in the day than I because most of the events they covered were afternoon or evening. Somehow, I knew them all well, though I can't tell you how anymore. I know that they often kept a six-pack of beer, or several, on the windowsill outside my office for after filing their stories. I think one of the sportswriters may have used my typewriter because I recall Carolyn Weldon cleaning it with some antiseptic soaked cloth in the morning. And I remember that Dave Bloss, who only weighed 120 pounds, came and went through my window because at one point he'd said he was never going through the "Mirrow" front door again. (Another sportswriter, Dennis Gildea, had made the "Mirrow" a popular alternative name for the newspaper in his humor column authored under the byline, T. Wes Brillik.)

As I settled in, I began to publish a recipe once a week. Some probably came from the wire service, others what I'd made up and used at home. Some of those that were not mine led to humor columns. One recipe said, "Correct the seasonings," and another, "make a blond roux." That led to a column in which I said, "You'd think they could get the seasoning right before publishing the recipe." And, "What's a blond roux? Is that anything like a brunette roue?" Some readers were amused, which encouraged me to keep on with humor columns. This was not difficult because my family and I had recently moved to "Sara's farm" in Rebersburg and I had lots of material, from dealing with three goats when they got in my car to looking for the septic tank and problems with the spring water when an animal died near the pipeline. The goats provided the most stories though. I took Esmerelda to be bred with a friend's billy goat but he rejected Esmerelda. (To this day my kids won't eat goat cheese because "it tastes like Esmerelda smelled.") Later I got Rebecca, already pregnant. She had Babette shortly thereafter. I had intended to milk Rebecca (goats' milk was all the rage for a while among us almost-hippies.) but I didn't have a stanchion to keep her upright for milking. She'd just lie down. I wrote, "You can't get milk from a lying down goat!!" Some of my early humor attempts were crude compared to what I learned to do in later years, but readers liked them and responded accordingly. That's how "Straight from Nature" was born. The goats, Esmerelda, Rebecca and Babette, provided material for many columns. There were other animal stories, too. I remember when our neighbors butchered three pigs. I got there after the actual butchering, when the women had gone off to make sausage and the men were standing around a big kettle cooking scrapple. I crawled into the bed of my pickup with my camera and just waited. Pretty soon everybody forgot I was there. They started joking around. One of the men pinned a pig tail to the back of another guy's pants; a man standing next to the scrapple kettle eating an apple tossed in the core when he was finished; and another man stuck a pig's tail so that it hung from the front of his fly. I got pictures of it all, though some wouldn't have been appropriate for newspaper publishing back in the day. I think I still have those negatives, too.

The Saturday paper always had a section devoted to church schedules and similar news as well as a picture of some local church. They used to send me out to take a picture for the allotted space, which was easy with my long lens. And somehow I was always able to bring back a picture that was the right shape for where it was supposed to run.

I wrote about my Amish neighbors, too, but never included a photo because they did not want to be photographed. As I recall, it had something to do with being against their religion, though I can't say why. However, I could take pictures of their animals, buildings, horses and buggies. Paul's store in Rebersburg had a rail in front for hitching the horses.

I got a good column about the store, too, because when he weighed produce he used a flashlight to read the numbers. After reading that column, he explained why he did that. Wish I remembered.

Just as I was beginning to feel settled, things started to change. I didn't know the details, nor, I believe, did the rest of the staff. But one day Paul Houck was gone. No explanation. People from the Altoona Mirror, parent company, began to move in with Marge Helsel in charge, The Mirror was owned by the Holtzinger family; Marge was a daughter of patriarch J.E. Holtzinger. They knew the newspaper business, but some young relative (Joe Jr.) with no newspaper experience moved into Houck's office. Carolyn Weldon said she'd met Houck downtown and he told her this was a low point in his life.

As I recall, Dave Cuzzolina became editor in the summer of 1976. Fay had left because he had high blood pressure problems. We knew he was gone for good because he took his pica stick with him. (I still have mine.) And Sheila Irvine, who temporarily replaced Fay, would soon leave to take a better job with another paper.

I should probably mention at this point that sex was an ever-present issue with the staff — young, unmarried men and women, rivalry and raging hormones. I remember some more specific details but I won't go into them here, except to note that even with this distraction, everybody got their jobs done on time — on deadline. I was less affected because I was a little older, and married. The sports guys called me, "Mrs. Robinson." If you saw the movie, you'll get it. I had two teenage daughters and I remember fretting about leaving them alone when my husband and I went away. Paul Mueller, whose only job, as far as I know, was to type obituaries, heard me. Mueller had a slight stutter. He said, "I'll babysit. Come on, girls, s-s-shower time!" Also, he'd occasionally write a parody of my column, "Strayed from Nature." I remain in touch with him and he's still as off-the-wall quirky as ever.

I published one controversial piece. A young woman I knew brought me what she had written about picking up a hitchhiker who tried to abduct her. I don't recall many details, but somehow she pulled over and attracted the attention of a couple who trained Penn State gymnasts. The young man was arrested. She ended her account, "How do you thank someone who saved your life?" I ran it exactly as she wrote it, in a special box. Dave Fay called me and shouted, "You have just fixed it so that man can never get a fair trial."

This rattled me because my page went pretty much as I set it. Nobody on staff had challenged the piece either before or after it was published. Looking for some reassurance, I guess, I actually called Jerry Weinstein at the Centre Daily Times for an opinion. He said he wished he had thought of it himself and I was feeling better until I learned that he told somebody things were so bad at the Mirror I had to call him for advice. I should have known better.

As business faltered, the Mirrow went to tabloid size, published twice a week. Terry Nau wrote a hed for his story: "Looking for the scores?" And went on to suggest there would not be any. That was his last day there. I'm sure he knew it would be. He called the diminished newspaper a "feature sheet" that lacked real news stories. Features were what I did best and I didn't have to spend all my time in the office or lay out pages anymore. I just went out with my camera and got pictures and stores that fit into the feature category. Almost any story can be made into a feature, so that was not a problem.

I wrote about a man I encountered at a sidewalk market who was selling pottery he made. In interviewing him I found out he also repaired broken appliances, did gardening and odd jobs. In the picture I took of him holding up his pot, he's grinning big. I took several shots from different angles and he said, "I can tell you've taken a few pictures."

That story, and his big smile were the cover of the last issue of the Pennsylvania Mirror ever published. Alongside it, to the left was the piece by Marge Helsel, with FINIS in large letters as the hed. She wrote about seeing the end of an era "with a heavy heart."

My Mirrow year shaped my future in a lot of ways. When I ended up at the Salisbury Post about 20 years later, I could cover routine stories but did better at features, especially those about people who ordinarily received no attention in a newspaper. And my columns became popular enough, as did my food pages, to be continued on a freelance basis for a long time after I'd retired. The Mirrow was my high school; the Salisbury Post was my post-graduation. The pay was a lot better but I could not have done it without the formative years at the Mirrow!

CHAPTER 17
THE 'STAT MAN' COMETH

By David L. Baker

I fell in love with newspapers as a teenager and after my first real job in high school at the Centre Daily Times I thought I would work forever in newspapers. That dream didn't last too many years, but then again I never figured I would teach Associated Press style to aspiring collegiate journalists 40 years later either.

HE'S EVERYWHERE – Dave Baker worked for the CDT and then in Penn State's sports information office for many years. He remains an assistant athletic director at PSU.

My generation reportedly will be the last of the great newspaper readers. I always buy a newspaper when I'm out of town and I so enjoyed reading the London dailies when I was in England in March 2019. Now I have digital subscriptions, most recently to The Athletic, as daily newspapers struggle for their existence. Even the Centre Daily Times is no longer published locally and with such an early deadline, the "news" is almost two days old, and has been reported on time everywhere else, that it hardly seems to be a "daily" newspaper.

***

I was excited when the Pennsylvania Mirror debuted on Dec. 11, 1968, and State College suddenly had two daily newspapers. The Mirror was fresh and vibrant with color, modern graphics and a modern layout. And the Mirror staff were just as much characters as many other newspaper writers I knew then and would meet later, but they were different characters. And they all loved to have fun at their jobs, before, during and after their work.

Okay, they were more bombastic, beginning with original sports editor Dave Fay, who loved ice hockey and had served in sports information at Rensselaer Polytechnic Institute (a college hockey power) before coming to State College. Dave was a loud and forceful personality who soon became city editor of the Mirror. Bill Greene replaced Dave and served a short stint as sports editor. He was succeeded in 1972 by Terry Nau, who also could be loud and boisterous but never threatening. I admired Terry because he had served in the Vietnam War. Many of my generation relied on student deferments and never wanted any part of that war, but he lived through it and never really talked about it — at least to me.

The Mirror added another sportswriter, Glenn Sheeley, in 1973. He would stay for one year before moving on to Pittsburgh and covering the Steelers for their first two Super Bowl championship seasons. The Mirror replaced Sheeley with Dave Bloss, who was not a loud personality. I remember Dave as a clever writer, kind and caring. Meanwhile, the CDT was fighting back with a strong but undermanned staff led by Ron Bracken, Doug McDonald and, in 1974, Gary Tuma.

For the Mirror, Dennis Gildea created the immortal columnist T. Wes Brillik from a Lewis Carroll line in Jabberwocky. Only those very close to the Mirror family knew T. Wes's true identity.. That Dennis would later become a writing teacher was never a surprise to me. He subsequently worked at the CDT but always impressed me as someone who would be a successful teacher. Dennis finished his career with 25 years as a journalism professor at Springfield College in Western Ma. J.D. Andrews, part of one of my favorite stories, which I will mention later, seemed to handle a lot of roles. He truly loved gymnastics and Penn State's coach, Gene Wettstone. I spent more time with J.D. later when I worked with the Penn State sports information office and handled Olympic sports.

Two newspapers offered Centre County a fresh perspective. I remember CDT editor Jerome Weinstein poring daily over the upstart Mirror to see if his staff has missed any important news coverage, and that rarely happened. The Mirror had a freshness and a different perspective, but just was not ingrained enough in the local business community and the whole of Centre County to sustain a long-term existence. The Mirror ceased publication on Dec. 31, 1977.

CDT advertising bosses Gene Reilly and Steve Braver had locked up the business and advertising market in the county, and the CDT writers covered all the governmental meetings, all the school boards, and all the community news so thoroughly that the Mirror could not break that stranglehold. I remember a fun summer working in the CDT Bellefonte office that was just another reminder of how entrenched the older newspaper was. The Mirror faced an uphill struggle from the start, but it was still a sad day when publication ended.

***

I never imagined that a summer job as a Little League scorekeeper would begin my love for newspapers, writing and editing, and a life-long career. A several-year stint at the Nittany Valley Little League at Gill Field off West College Avenue, now marked only with a small "Gill Field" sign to serve as a reminder for the Young Boys of Summer in State College, was my start.

I worked out of a stable but not massive equipment-and-scorer shed above and behind home plate. I was always interested in sports statistics, probably because I was such a good field-no hit second baseman several years earlier in the same league, so I would post batting average leaders, pitching leaders, and other statistical leaders on the outside shed wall every night when I came to the field. And that was in the days before computers and before I learned to type, so my stats were all handwritten and hand-calculated.

After the game, I would drop off the Centre Daily Times box score form at the Fraser Street office because the CDT ran full box scores – just like the Big Leagues! – for the players and families to check out in the next day's afternoon paper. One day in my second or third year, sports editor Doug McDonald stopped me early in the season and asked if I would be interested in a summer job, helping answer the phones and take box scores over the phone from the other county Little Leagues. He mentioned something about my good penmanship and how my box scores always "added up." One thing led to another and soon I was writing one- or two-paragraph stories, traveling out to Cain Field in Pleasant Gap and covering fast-pitch softball tournaments (where I was volunteered into being the tournament scorekeeper). In college, I started covering high school football games of Centre County schools, from fields at West Branch High School to Mount Union High School. Here I was interviewing the real gentlemen who were the local high school coaches after games, compiling statistics and writing stories with a byline.

Eventually, the CDT moved its editorial offices to the back of the building. The entrance to the newsroom, sports department, and editor Jerome Weinstein's office were off the back alley. One summer I was taking a late-morning class at Penn State and I was asked if I would like to come early in the morning, write sports headlines and make/suggest adjustments in the layout of the sports pages if the Associated Press news stories provided good overnight stories. That was really heady stuff for someone who just had switched his major from mathematics to journalism.

This opportunity provided me a great education to work with the quirky, but dedicated CDT news writers, and with managing editor Bill Welch and news editor Tom Berner. It was also a great time to be working with newspapers, because it was the Watergate Era and every time the bell rang on the AP wire machine it was likely a new Watergate development. One day just before publication, the AP bell rang and the story of vice president Spiro Agnew's resignation ran, the front page of day's CDT was re-plated and the Agnew story was on Page One. Somewhere in an old box in my home I have the three pieces of hot metal type and the headline "Agnew Resigns." There was nothing quite like the excitement of a newsroom when big news came in on the teletype machine.

***

This fall marks my 50th year working Penn State football games. That's 46 years with the Penn State athletic department and four years as an undergraduate at Penn State. A lot of games, a lot of hours and a lot of memories.

I've been asked several times if I plan to write a book when I retire and I've considered that. But I could not write a kiss-and-tell book as too many memories and stories would be out of context to try to explain, most of them falling in-the you-had-to-here-to-understand. Once in a while, I'm asked to list my 10 favorite athletic events in which I've been involved or worked, and again, there's always a back story or an aftermath to the event that changed my perception, but I do have that list. Some of those events and reasons involved persons from other schools, including one I've been asked about from a writer of a book about Pitt football, but I'm not willing to embarrass anyone at this point. I'll detail two of them here, and one involves friends from the Pennsylvania Mirror.

Any long-time observer of Penn State athletics would list the school's and Joe Paterno's first national championship in the Superdome in New Orleans on January 1, 1983, against Georgia, as a top 10 moment, and of course that's No. 1 on my list. Some of the memories before the game and after the game shape my opinion:

- Quarterback Todd Blackledge's introduction of his starting offensive team aired before the game and it was taped on the practice field on Saturday morning several weeks in advance by the ABC crew, led by sideline reporter Jim Lampley, who has enjoyed a distinguished broadcasting career at the Olympics, with boxing, and on the West Coast. Today, the Centre Daily Times and other Pennsylvania sportswriters, TV stations and other film crews might be invited and might record the session from the sidelines of that taping, but in December 1982, it was a private session —and that made it all the more memorable for me. Todd introduced each of his starting offensive lineup, most with jokes and some slightly risqué comments. I actually invited 12 starters because Kenny Jackson, Gregg Garrity and the late Kevin Baugh rotated at wide receiver and I didn't want to slight anyone. Kenny no-showed and it worked out to perfection when Todd introduced Kevin as the "winner of the recent ET look-alike contest" and his eyes opened wide at the comment and he did look like the title character of Stephen Spielberg's movie. The first take was almost perfect and the time was incredible, several seconds over the prescribed time limit. The director and crew were shaking their heads at how great the first filming was and decided to go one more take. Just as perfect the second time around and Lampley turned to me and said, "Some day he (Blackledge) is going to have my job." That prediction proved correct as Todd developed into a top-notch network college football analyst, mostly with ABC and ESPN.
- Blackledge's touchdown pass to Garrity was the game-winner and all Penn Staters remember the catch that was captured for posterity on the Sports Illustrated cover. I remember Blackledge talking Paterno out of a safe run on third-and-too-many-yards late in the game and then throwing a sideline out completion for a first down to keep the ball away from Georgia. I remember Blackledge leading the postgame locker room celebration with victory cigars and then walking down the relative

emptiness of the back hallways of the Superdome to the press conference with Joe Paterno telling me and no one else, "Dave, they will never be able to take this one away from me." My sports information compadre Mary Jo Haverbeck and I drove safety Mark Robinson, the last player to appear at the press conference, back to the Sheraton in a rainstorm, arrived at the hotel with the party still on downstairs and we all headed to the service elevators to our rooms. Exhausted would have a mild word to describe me at 3 a.m. or whenever it was, and I entered my suite (well, actually a room with a large sitting area), only to find my wife and all the sportswriters from Pennsylvania — Pittsburgh, Philadelphia, Harrisburg, Lancaster, Allentown, State College — enjoying snacks, soft drinks and adult beverages in my room. So, much for the thought of sleep.

- The night after the game the travel party returned to Harrisburg and then bused back to the football offices on campus. All along the old route back to State College, local fire trucks turned out to honk their horns and escort buses through their jurisdictional areas. Families and many little children came out to their mailboxes at the side of the road to wave their flashlights or shake their cowbells. It was an incredible victory parade for 90 miles back to another celebration on campus. Anyone who was on the team and official party buses that night will never forget how much that national championship meant to the state of Pennsylvania and Penn State fans.

Some national championships are won much closer to home, including a very special one in Philadelphia.

Any listing of the icons of the Penn State athletic history would include gymnastics coach Gene Wettstone and if ever a Mount Rushmore of the legendary coaches was carved into Mount Nittany, Gene was a lock to be featured.

Gene crammed a lifetime of accomplishments through his 100th birthday in 2013, the year that he died. In 36 years in Happy Valley he established a world-recognized gymnastics program with nine

NCAA championships, many individual champions and 13 Olympians. He coached the U.S. Olympic team but his forte was organization and logistics, so he was the Olympic team manager many times, bringing his flair for the event to Rec Hall with many spectacular international meets. The Russian national team appeared in Rec Hall at the height of the Cold War and so did the great Japanese team; ABC's Wide World of Sports broadcast these Wettstone spectaculars to a national television audience.

Gene was a showman but he was very particular about the details and rarely delegated until you could prove that you were up to his high standards. It took me a while to reach the level, but I was proud when he allowed me to be a part of the gymnastics program when I was the assistant SID.

In 1976, the Nittany Lions had not won a national title in 10 years but were one of the favorites when the NCAA meet was held at McGonigle Hall in Philadelphia. That was before the event could be followed on the Internet with live scoring. Temple didn't have the scoreboard capability to keep fans up to date on the score.

So, we improvised. J.D. Andrews and Dennis Gildea, both of the Mirror staff, and I each took one corner of the area and we kept track of the top teams' individual scorers, tossed out the low scores, and kept our own running tally. It was a lot of work but a lot of excitement when the Nittany Lions led by parallel bars champ and future Olympian Gene Whelan captured Penn State's ninth championship under Wettstone, in what would be his final season.

The post-championship celebration is a faded memory, although I remember driving to the local grocery store located across the street from the team hotel. I stocked up on water, soft drinks, ice, snacks, fruit and whatever and dashed back to Wettstone's hotel room to stock the bathtub with the drinks and set up the food and snacks for a team party.

I don't remember if J.D. or Dennis came by, but they deserved to enjoy that celebration after one of Penn State's most memorable championships.

CHAPTER 18
THE MIRROR SHATTERS

By Dave Cuzzolina

(Editor's note: Dave Cuzzolina was city editor of the Mirror from September 1976 through Dec. 31, 1977.)

As I recall my brief time at the Pennsylvania Mirror, it's somewhat fitting that I do so in the midst of a pandemic, with the world in turmoil over Covid-19, insecurity governing people's day-to-day lives.

Now, to say the Mirror was in turmoil would be overstating it. A bit. Clearly, though, insecurity, caused by the paper's consistent inability to sustain itself financially and the loss of three respected leaders, had exacted a heavy toll.

PERSPECTIVE – Dave Cuzzolina can look back on his experience with the Pennsylvania Mirror and smile

When a business struggles financially, rumors of doom will arise and spread. In newspapers, it's a fire nearly impossible to contain. Unlike most other businesses, a paper can't hide its numbers. Its "books," so to speak, are there for anyone to see. Every day. It didn't take a CPA to tote up the Mirror's advertising inches and do the math.

The fire burned white hot with the departure of the three

men referenced above: Publisher Blair Bice, Executive Editor Paul Houck and City Editor Dave Fay. Morale teetered on the edge. Some people had shut down. Anger got the better of others.

Anyone toting a duffel bag stuffed full of optimism into such an atmosphere suffers a culture shock. Added to the expected challenges in a newspaper editor's job—personnel issues, lack of resources, angry readers, etc.—it made for a bumpy ride.

Not that my year and a half as editor was all bad. It was not. I also saw a pride and determination to maintain the paper's quality standards in spite of all the noise. The news staff responded well; sports maintained its award-winning ways, and we had a few wins and fun along the way. We ignored the rumors. What else could we do?

Until the day the rumors stopped being rumors.

Then came the toughest task I would face, one my rose-colored glasses blinded me to, kept me from even considering. I would have to give the corpse of this once-proud newspaper a proper burial.

***

The Altoona Mirror hired me as a general assignment reporter right from college, with no journalism education or experience. I thought they were crazy, but I wasn't arguing. I wanted to write, and everything I'd read about the craft said if you wanted to be good at it, write every day. A daily newspaper seemed to fit the bill quite nicely. I reported to managing editor Bob Boyer the day after Labor Day 1972 and settled in to my desk. I remember looking at my typewriter and thinking what a thrill it was that I would be paid for using it.

I was 21 years old.

In those days, the Altoona Mirror published a six-day-a-week evening paper with a circulation in the mid-30s and a newsroom staff of about 25, including news and sports reporters, lifestyle, obits, a regional desk, four photographers, a three-person city desk and a wire editor. Meeting the staff that first day I noticed only a few younger coworkers. People in their 20s. Eventually, I became aware of a sister paper in State College called the Pennsylvania Mirror. The person telling me about it rolled his eyes more than once as he did. I had to know more. Claiming no direct knowledge of the situation, he called what he told me "scuttlebutt."

It went like this: The Pennsylvania Mirror fulfilled a dream of Altoona Mirror publisher J.E. "Ted" Holtzinger of owning a newspaper in State College, the home of Penn State, one of his great loves. My coworker claimed to know that the younger paper had never been self-sustaining financially, the money to launch it and keep it afloat being siphoned off the significant profits in Altoona.

As a result, the Pennsylvania Mirror was computers and cold type and crisp offset printing. Altoona was manual typewriters and hot lead and outmoded letterpress. State College produced a colorful, exciting newspaper, sweeping statewide quality awards with consistency, while Altoona slogged along, the forgotten child, the "old, gray Mirror."

This disparity, I discovered, triggered strong emotions among my younger coworkers. The more I learned, the more I shared their resentment that the money being shoveled into what they saw as an incinerator in State College should be used to upgrade the very successful Altoona paper instead.

At the same time, as journalists, we couldn't help admiring the Pennsylvania Mirror. We even tried to wring some pride out of it being a sister paper, albeit Cinderella to the Altoona Mirror's haggy step-sister. And truth be told, more than one of us harbored a desire to be part of it.

But it hung on, and I would be more than OK with that because in four short years the owners would offer me the city editor's job there. Once again I thought they were crazy. Once again I wasn't arguing. I don't know what they saw in an English lit major with no formal journalism training, my only experience being four years of reporting. All I'd managed to that point in my life was a checkbook.

But I didn't flinch. They gave me the opportunity of a lifetime.

And a life line.

I had abandoned the Altoona Mirror and journalism after four years for a public relations writing job at Penn State. Restless, I saw P.R. as an opportunity to spread my wings a little. And who didn't want to work for Penn State, right?

Almost immediately I missed the newsroom. A daily newspaper shoots excitement directly into your veins. I wanted to dig for important stories again instead of having fluffy ones handed to me. Huddled in my own small office in cavernous Old Main, I yearned for the camaraderie, the banter, the clacking of twenty manual typewriters at once, and from time to time the frantic bell-clanging of the UPI teletype machines screaming, "Something urgent has happened in the world, you better come look!"

So, for me, the opportunity to return to newspapers and lead a first-class newsroom like the Pennsylvania Mirror's was an offer I couldn't refuse.

It was the summer of '76 and I was 25.

I recall no one mapping out my mission for me, nor me asking. That's not to say they didn't, or I didn't. I just don't remember. Looking back, I probably thought my task was obvious: Pull the paper from financial quicksand, and as quickly as possible. The bottom of the hourglass was filling up fast. Altoona was a family-owned company, and word on the street pointed to a growing concern among some family members about the cost of keeping the paper on life-support.

It could have been ego or naiveté, in hindsight probably both, but I approached the challenge with confidence. In my last days at PSU I spent more time on the Mirror job than I did for the university, planning with enthusiasm, eager to get started.

The Pennsylvania Mirror's sports section was its strong suit, and sports meant a lot in State College. I figured they didn't need my leadership, which worked out well because early on and to a man they made it clear they didn't want it. We would engage in a few tiffs along the way but for the most part, for the next year and a half, before we knew it had a fancy name or useful purpose, we practiced social distancing.

I couldn't dwell on that situation. I set it aside, concentrated on the news side, where I saw more opportunities anyway. The goal would be to cover the hell out of local news, let the circulation department make people notice, and facilitate the ad department's job. Looking back, it all seems so naive.

Fortunately, the news reporters accepted me. They seemed eager for a fresh start. I think they would have been happy with any port in a storm after the management upheaval. It seemed to affect them more than concerns about the paper closing. Young and short-tenured, most if not all knew their futures lay outside State College. It was a stepping stone. It didn't matter how slippery it was.

They bought into the coverage plan almost immediately. With their input we arranged and rearranged beats and kept everything within Centre County, home of the most likely readers. Even if this "circle the wagons" approach had been tried before, I could think of nothing that made more sense.

Covering one county and the university proved a challenge with only four or five reporters (further experience would teach me you never have the number you want), but we managed to land on a workable phase one. Much fine-tuning would follow.

We still covered the dreaded municipal and school board meetings but did not let them interfere with more in-depth reporting and analysis stories that could set us apart, always basing our news judgment decisions on impact and interest. And I think "news you can use" was a catch-phrase back then.

So armed, we set out to slay Goliath. Or at least steal a sustainable piece of his pie. We competed with the CDT every day (whether they knew it or not), and by virtue of being an AM paper we would beat them to most stories, provided we found them, so we concentrated on finding them.

Personally, though I missed reporting, I loved being back in a newsroom. The noisy, hammering clacks of manual typewriters were now the barely audible whimpers of taps on keyboards. Still, the atmosphere was charged, exciting. Being the underdog gave us a common enemy and a cause to rally around. And when we scooped the CDT, we shared in the childish joy of tweaking our competitor's nose.

As life returned to normal in the newsroom, the rumors seemed to lose momentum. When one did arise, my advice was to ignore it. What else could we do, really? We couldn't control it. We were doing a job. We were having fun.

Until one day the rumors stopped being rumors.

***

Before I address the Pennsylvania Mirror's final days, I feel compelled, being its last editor, to contribute my two cents to the discussion of why the experiment failed. Just opinion, based on a relatively short stay there. Others will have a deeper, clearer insight.

Perhaps it was ill-conceived, doomed from the start. The name suggests aspirations far beyond Centre County. In fact, the front page of the first issue shouted "Good Morning Central Pennsylvania" in huge type. Names of communities large, small and microscopic, in both Centre and Blair, littered the page like ants on a picnic blanket under the rather generic nameplate.

Maybe a State College Mirror or Centre County Mirror, with a more practical, compact coverage area, focused from the get-go on news relevant to people most likely to subscribe, would have fared better.

Or maybe the Centre Daily Times held the county too firmly in its grip and would have kept its dominant status no matter what Altoona threw at it.

Regardless, I believe J.E. Holtzinger deserves applause for the effort. He believed in the Pennsylvania Mirror. Conventional wisdom held that after years of losses only he stood between it and oblivion. That he died in 1977 and the paper closed at the end of that year proved it for me.

His pet project provided a lot of good young journalists with a launching pad for successful careers. With Penn State University to draw from, eager and excellent job candidates lined up to get in.

Terry Nau, in his piece for this book, has described the very successful post-Mirror careers of many of the sportswriters.

On the news side I am confined to those whom I came across in my less than two years. Reporters Jim Elder, Nancy Adams, Sara Pitzer (lifestyle), Don Hopey, Dave Shaffer, Janet Kelly, Paul Mueller, Becky Bennett; photographers Bill Wallace and Dave Hamilton. (Sincerest apologies to anyone I've forgotten.) I know Jim, Don, Sara and Becky went on to bigger, better things in journalism and communications. I have to believe the others did, too. They were too good not to have.

Saving the best for last, in my opinion the finest all-around journalist on staff when I arrived was Sheila Irvine, a fellow Altoonan. Thank God for her. If I could dedicate this chapter to anyone, it would be Sheila. She filled the empty editor's seat commendably on an interim basis until I arrived. In corresponding with a former colleague about this book I was reminded of something I had forgotten but found hilarious at the time. For 11 straight days she put a color photo of an animal on page one. Sheila loved animals. I'm betting a lot of readers loved them, too.

SHEILA IRVINE
... best of the bunch

It illustrated the freedom with which the Mirror operated, not bound by convention but fresh and lively, not your grandfather's newspaper.

I felt it inappropriate to ask so I never knew if Sheila wanted the editor's job and was passed over, or it was offered and she turned it down. If the former, she showed no signs of what would have been understandable bitterness. At 30 years old, with a decade of diverse journalism experience, she had way more credentials than I for the job, her veteran status there not the least of them.

Anyway, she took me under her kindhearted wing and held my hand through the arduous process of getting to know the ropes — the newspaper, the newsroom staff, the rest of the people in the building, cold-type processes, the region, and the history that shaped the paper's unsteady internal dynamics.

I leaned on her hard for support. She never failed me, seemed to dip into a bottomless vat of patience, and remained always helpful.

I remember her suffering through a horrible stretch of time. She loathed capital punishment, found it barbaric, and during our days together at the Mirror a convicted murderer named Gary Mark Gilmore made headlines by demanding his death sentence be carried out. On Jan. 17, 1977, at 8:07 a.m. his wish was granted, by firing squad at a state prison in Draper, Utah.

A distraught Sheila, in the days leading up to the scheduled execution, shed tears openly. The day of the execution she missed work for the first time since my arrival. It would also be the only time.

For me, Sheila's reaction demonstrated her limitless capacity for empathy and compassion. She cared about people, loved animals, respected all life.

After several months riding shotgun with me on the city desk, she left for greener, more stable pastures. Knowing her and the love she had for the Pennsylvania Mirror and her unflagging sense of loyalty, she wanted to go much sooner. She stayed to ensure my readiness to fly solo, putting her own needs second behind those of the paper.

In trying to locate Sheila for this memoir I found her obituary. She died in 2012, after a career as a reporter for the York Dispatch, Harrisburg Patriot and the Florida Times-Union.

Her online obit read in part, "She was a strong woman who always stood up for what she believed in. Since childhood, Sheila presented a strong defense for people she saw as disabled, in need, or hurt. She took care of others who were less fortunate than her."

That was the Sheila I was fortunate to have by my side in State College in the late 1970s. She hadn't changed. No surprise. A tribute left for the family on the funeral home site read: "Sheila was my sister's mother in law. Our family will always be better because she was a member of it."

She had a son and I'll go out on a limb and say she made a great mom.

To me, in many ways, she epitomized the heart and soul of the Pennsylvania Mirror, at least during my time with her.

Sheila was 65 when she died.

Though her leaving saddened me at the time, I would later be glad she missed witnessing the Mirror's demise from the inside. The end, neither quick nor painless, would have been sheer agony for her.

When Mr. Holtzinger died in January 1977, I think she saw the writing on the wall before any of us. In late summer of that year, the publication was changed to a tabloid and the publishing schedule to twice a week, Wednesdays and Saturdays. It could have been a "Hail Mary" effort to salvage a piece of the market. Maybe a bean counter somewhere figured the new arrangement would be sustainable. Or maybe someone thought a protracted exit would be more graceful. No matter. It accomplished none of that.

I didn't ask questions. I should have. Maybe I could have talked them out of it. It was not the way the Pennsylvania Mirror should have taken its final bow. The tabloid served no purpose for news or sports or readers except to tarnish a legacy, the way a champion boxer who goes one fight too many might be remembered as overweight and out of shape.

She deserved a better fate.

The merciful end came Dec. 31, 1977. I can't say I remember specifics about putting the final issue to bed. I recall no embraces or tears the night the last one of us out the door switched off the lights for the last time. What I do recall is a sense of relief, like when a loved one dies after a long illness and you know they're better off.

Personally, I struggled with the failure. I had let a lot of people down. Ownership, readers, all the employees who lost their jobs. And myself. As years passed I forgave myself, recognizing my naiveté and coming to realize Ben Bradlee couldn't have saved it.

After the closing, I returned to the Altoona Mirror and in 1985 became managing editor. Unfortunately, two years earlier the family had sold to Thomson Newspapers, whose smell for milking its products dry still lingers today.

Interestingly, the company tried in the late 1980s to improve its image. At an editor-publisher conference in Nashville around 1988 nobody was allowed to mention the "P" word (profit). The rapture lasted until the bean counters saw the first dip in the bottom line. Like one fiscal quarter.

Burned out after seven years of that, looking for a less hectic career, I returned to P.R., where hectic became frantic. For a local hospital I managed communications through three mergers and a nurses strike. The final merger made the hospital a UPMC facility. When the opportunity to retire via a buyout presented itself in 2015, at age 64, I called it a career.

Hard to believe my Pennsylvania Mirror days were more than 40 years ago. I still wonder what they saw in a 25-year-old English lit major still wet behind the ears by journalism standards, and I still think they were crazy.

But honest to God, because of the high points and despite the low points, I'd give anything to go back and do it all again. How crazy is that?

HAVING FUN – Mirror sportswriters Chance Conner and Dave Bloss enjoy a light moment in the newsroom with news reporter Nancy Jane Adams. (Pa. Mirror photo)

CHAPTER 19
THESE WERE GOOD PEOPLE

By Dave Bloss - Mirror sportswriter

Okay. Somebody has to stay behind and do the obits.

Let's start with the **Pennsylvania Mirror** itself. When it cut back to twice-a-week publication just before football season began in 1977, you could hear the death rattle. As is the case all across America today, all incentive to buy the newspaper or advertise in it simply died.

We had fallen into the habit of still covering all the sports, but only coming into the Benner Pike office the two days a week when we were actually producing the paper. This disappointed our Altoona Mirror overseers, but we knew we could make our deadlines without hanging around all week.

About that final deadline. When we wandered into the office on a late December early afternoon, we were told this was the last edition and then it would all be over.

The sports department wrote whatever stories were in our made-of-paper notebooks and began designing and producing pages.

But as early evening approached, enthusiasm began to wane. Chance Conner and I lasted until about 8 pm, then headed to the downtown bars. In a typical Mirror misread of finances, we had recently been given a hundred or so business cards. We handed them out and anyone who got one had the distinct honor of buying us a drink.

JOHN ANDREWS
... *deadline wizard*

John Andrews, the editor who put thousands of Mirrors to bed, was a man of routine in everything he did in his life. There was a time and a place and a way of doing something, and that was how it would be done.

Every journalist, backroom page builder, pressroom operator and circulation driver just wanted to get that night over with. Why stick around?

I could use a cosmic fact checker on this, but I believe the last story John put into the newspaper was the Astro-Bluebonnet Bowl. USC 47, Texas A&M 28. Plus the game statistics in agate type. Why? Because it was the latest possible news he could get into the newspaper and make deadline. That was the routine, and why would that night be any different?

A few days later, there was one last trip to the office to clean out the desks. Once again showing that special Mirror financial acumen, we carried garbage bags full of college and pro football media guides out to the dumpster. They are now worth about their weight in gold on eBay. Our work done, we moved on to the unemployment office, where most of us discovered the state of Pennsylvania would pay us $9 a week more not to work than the Mirror had been paying us for whatever you would call what we had been doing.

As the years went by, it remained easy to stay in touch with the man of routine. John still only answered the phone if he heard the exact ring twice — hang it up — ring again sequence that allowed him to ignore 99 percent of the outside world. He never moved from the second-floor walk-up in Centre Hall that he rented sometime in the Sixties and maybe one time moved the couch two inches to the left.

What also never changed was what a joy it was to meet him for a beer or two. John passed in 2017.

Chance Conner was our entree to the State College Little Lions. A graduate of the Class of 1970, Chance was the only one of us who could answer yes to the immortal Central Pennsylvania question: "Yins local?"

Like the rest of us, Chance was attracted to the excesses made possible by the Mirror schedule and lifestyle. There was an assignment (God, who thought this up?) to talk to tailgaters who came down from Syracuse. Rather than return to the office, he climbed in one of their vehicles and traveled many miles north before the haze began clearing and he asked to get out. That story ran a day late and did not at all resemble what really happened.

In the midst of all this frivolity, Chance would often turn serious and ask out loud what we were doing and what was the meaning of all this? He wrestled with it even after he moved on to Denver. First he wrote a screenplay that was fairly accurate, but the main character was a cross between Chance and God. (Constructive criticism, naturally poorly taken.) He trimmed it down to a novel that was supposed to be the first of a trilogy.

Chance passed in 2010. According to a tribute story in the Denver Post, "His career as a reporter and editor spanned more than 30 years, including work at the Colorado Daily, Boulder Daily Camera, Rocky Mountain News, USA Today, Centre Daily Times and Winter Park Manifest.

"He was a terrific reporter. He just got things quickly," said Mike McPhee, a former Post staffer and Conner colleague. "He had a reporter's sense of how things fit together."

Conner also taught writing and tutored students at Metropolitan State College of Denver and Community College of Denver.

Dave Fay was the ringleader. Nice resume: born in Catholic suburban Boston, moved to Warren, Pa., in his teens, joined the Navy instead of finishing high school, somehow ended up in the

HOCKEY WRITER –
Dave Fay went from the Mirror to the Hockey Hall of Fame before his death in 2007.

Virgin Islands and got a newspaper job, returned to Warren to work for the local newspaper, found a job as a sports information director at RPI, moved into a job with the Penn State sports information department, was moved out of that job when a football road trip to UCLA went off the rails. Perfect training to run the Mirror, where he began as sports editor before moving up to city editor.

He sat at the wide desk in the back of the newsroom, hair and face somehow turning even redder as he screamed orders and obscenities. It might have been intimidating if he hadn't often had his sleepy pet beagle tied under his desk — or on at least one occasion his toddler twin sons.

He was a newsman. He quickly figured out that the hundreds of truckers protesting up on Interstate 80 was a big deal and not just a C.W. McCall "Convoy" song. Not every tip which maybe was obtained on a barstool panned out. He roared into the office one afternoon and screamed that Patty Hearst had been sighted and we had to find her first. He sent me to Tyrone. Never figured that town was high on Patty's list.

Dave worked a double shift. Into the office in the early afternoon and stay until the news pages were finished about midnight. Then a fast car ride to the bars before they closed. Earlier in this book, Mr. Emmers gives a fine description of the My-O-My bar. Dave favored the corner table, big enough for when a celebrity like Richie Hebner or Jimmy Breslin was holding court, and close enough to monitor the tiny room to the left where the strippers changed, and the bathrooms to the right where the drunk gays from the front bar met the drunk rednecks from the back bar. Owner Jack Sapia was 40 years ahead of his time when it came to marketing sexual confusion, and Dave watched it all and laughed.

At 1:45 am, Sapia was legally allowed to sell two six-packs to go as enticement to get people out the doors. Fay and his 12 new friends would most often lead us to wherever he was living. That shift, which was too much beer, too much talk, and too much loud ABBA on the eight-track, could last until 7 am. It was great.

He got out before it was too late. He took a job at the University Heights liquor store, perhaps the greatest fox in the hen house story ever. Then it was back to journalism, running a newsroom in Pawtucket, RI. I joined him there in 1979 and Terry Nau soon followed. There was an Elks lodge bar in the basement of the same building. We'll just leave it at that.

One day Dave came to me and whispered: "The Washington Times needs a sportswriter. Should I do it?" Work for the Moonies? Made perfect sense.

He did a helluva job in Washington. He covered the Redskins in their glory days, and was beloved by Joe Gibbs and the famous offensive line nicknamed the "Hogs." Then he switched to his true love of hockey and was all over the Capitals beat. Once again, everyone from the owner on down loved Dave. He would often call or write about players I had never heard of and combine it with invective about some competing Washington Post beat writer I had never read. It was great.

Tongue cancer got him, but the laughs continued long after the beer and cigarettes stopped and the operations began. Terry and I drove down to see him in May of 2007. The news of his selection to the Writers Wing of the Hockey Hall of Fame had just arrived. We watched the Preakness together on TV and even though it was starting to be a struggle to talk, he spent hours telling us about Capitals players we didn't know and Washington Post beat writers we didn't read. It was great.

He wrote one last e-mail telling me I was full of shit for some sports opinion I had shared. "You always made more sense drunk," he concluded. Words to live by, I guess.

Dave passed in 2007. In his name, the Capitals have raised huge money for cancer research.

That big news editor's desk had a small work space at one end for the assistant editor. **Sheila K. Irvine** was the bravest of souls to sit in that chair. Often the only woman who lasted through Fay's double shifts, she was a funny and decent soul surrounded for endless hours by newspaper mongrels.

Sheila saw the good in people, and she tried to see the good in news. At one point when she was serving as news editor, she took advantage of the high-quality Mirror color presses and for 11 days in a row put a huge photo of a cute animal on the front page. This was especially tricky at a time when the Vietnam War and Watergate were wrapping up and cute animals weren't exactly Breaking News. But she wasn't wrong.

Sheila went on to bigger papers and a happy family life. She passed in 2012.

Dennis Gildea loved stories.

The numbers on the scoreboards meant almost nothing to him. What mattered was how people acted and reacted. And since people mostly act badly, his catchphrase for them: "yellow dogs."

Dennis didn't just bring friends into the Mirror orbit. They came in bunches — the Tavern Restaurant waiters, the runners, the Clearfield wrestling gang. Often they would mix and match, and Dennis would watch and listen.

And he would chortle. That's the only word to describe the sound he emitted when something pleased him.

He chortled:
- when he saw Penn State cross country coach Harry Groves run an extension cord about a half-mile across the White

Course so the National Anthem could be played before an NCAA cross country championship. Groves was peeved because foreign-born runners were beginning to dominate.
- whenever someone new hated him as he predicted defeat yet again for the almost-never-losing Little Lions football team, adding for good measure that the cheerleaders were ugly.
- like any good Coaldale kid, whenever some wrestler from one of Pennsylvania's many godforsaken hills and hollows earned either PIAA or NCAA wrestling glory.
- whenever Tucker Arnold, one of Clearfield's finest, left cold six-packs on the window sill at the Mirror office, convinced we really needed them.

He chortled hardest at his own creation — a charity wrestling match at Bellefonte High School. The gym was jammed. Disc jockey/sportscaster and tight friend Todd Jeffers expected to wrestle Dennis. But Dennis graciously stepped aside, and onto the mat came John Hall, a hulking gentleman who had recently finished up

GOOD TEAMMATES – Dennis Gildea met his future wife, Constance Wicklund, late in his Mirror career.

a term at the Rockview State Correctional Institute just up the road. Jeffers survived getting slammed around and had a lifetime story.

It was a surprise that Dennis was better prepared than most of us when the Mirror died and all of a sudden we had to be someplace else. My someplace else was a used bookstore on College Avenue. Dennis walked in and took me straight to the then unknown John Irving and Fred Exley books — the good stories.

Turns out he had piled up enough credits during a 15-year on-and-off stab at academics to get hired to teach a beginning journalism course at Penn State.

The problem was attendance. We worked hard at the Mirror, but sometimes we failed to attend. Now he had a class on Wednesday afternoons. Our unemployment checks came early enough on Wednesday mornings for us to drink lunch at the Skellar.

That's when I found out he was a good teacher. One Wednesday when we already had a table full of empties, a delegation of his students came into the Skellar. "Please come teach us," they asked. Not yellow dogs.

Dennis eventually left State College and took a job teaching and advising the student newspaper at Marist. He lost that job because he defended his staff as a matter of principle when they were being pressured by faculty and fellow students.

He moved on to Springfield College in 1994, and built a career and a life in western Massachusetts. Not every student got him, but the good ones loved him. He'd invite me once a year to show his class what could happen to a person if they stayed in journalism. The best two or three kids would hang around afterward.

His stacked-to-the-roof office turned out to be the perfect cubbyhole for writing books. His best one — *Hoop Crazy: The Lives of Clair Bee and Chip Hilton* — took forever to write because he traveled for years to hear first-hand hundreds of stories about the basketball coach whose books taught a generation of boys how they should live and play.

Brain cancer got Dennis. At age 76, he was running near his house one day, and was knocked flat by the disease the next day.

It was the usual hell trying to get him the best treatment. There was one high-speed ambulance trip to the hospital in Springfield. Struggling to speak a couple days later, he told me: "The woman who was saving me? She's part-time. Two days a week she goes down to the Cape and counts sharks.

"Good story."

Dennis could never simply ask you for something. He would always say: "You'd be my best friend for life if you would ..."

Toward the end, when he needed a lot of help, he still said it and sort of smiled, well aware there was no longer much of a time commitment.

Dennis passed away on May 3, 2020, at age 77, with wife Constance and sister Mary at his side.

It was a good paper, these were good people, and there were good stories.

LONG JOURNEY – *Dave Bloss worked as sports editor of the Providence Journal for 13 years before finishing his career overseas, training young journalists in former Russian provinces.*

VINTAGE ERA – Bill Welch, front right, sits in the
Centre Daily Times newsroom in 1978,
amid the typewriters and copy paper of a bygone era.
(R Thomas Berner photo)

EPILOGUE: THE EULOGY

How many people get a chance in their waning years to reunite with people they knew 50 years ago? That's the feeling I got as I helped Terry Nau copy edit the chapters you've just read. Not only do I remember the people fondly, but I also remember many of the stories they retell in their chapters. And I remember the many people mentioned who are no longer with us—a list almost as long as the table of contents.

As journalists, we were lucky to be alive when we were. The technology changes alone are almost mind blowing. I started in a lead-based newspaper in a small town writing stories on a typewriter and now newspapers are assembled so efficiently with computers that a lot of the blue and white collar billets have disappeared. If your stories are set in type, for example, you don't need a typographer. Unfortunately, some newspaper companies even try to get by without editors.

The business has been good to most of us in this book, even if we have moved on to a career in something other than newspapers. Given that the number of newspapers has declined rapidly in our lifetime (two that I worked for disappeared and a third is on the ropes), moving on was a matter of survival. We're left with the memories.

This book is one of them.

~ R. Thomas Berner

www.ingramcontent.com/pod-product-compliance
Lightning Source LLC
Chambersburg PA
CBHW070139080526
44586CB00015B/1764